Cooking with

GOURMET GRAINS

2

author: Charlene S. Martinsen
book design and illustrations: Dustyn Schear/Magus design
photographic direction: Richard C. Runyon Design
photography: George de Gennaro
lithography: Farwest/Acme Inc.
For information on how to obtain additional copies write: Stone-Buhr
Kitchens, 4052 28th Ave. S.W., Seattle, Washington 98126

are made from whole grain. Whole grain products supply vitamins and minerals and they are exciting to use. They will add texture and contrast to the foods you prepare for your family.

This book contains some allergy recipes that can be included in milk, egg or wheat-free allergy diets. Recipes made with Stone-Buhr specialty flours are different from traditional recipes. Be sure to review the Allergy section in this book to give you a better idea of how to use these recipes.

The recipes have been placed on the pages in this book so that there will be room for you to make notes next to each recipe you prepare. You might want to note, next to a recipe you have tried, the addition of special seasonings your family prefers, the baking time in your oven, a special way to serve the dish, or menu ideas that you found especially successful.

Above all, I hope you will have fun cooking with Stone-Buhr products. Reacquainting your family with some of the oldest known food products of man, the grains, is an exciting experience. I know you will discover ways to use these grains. I hope you will share your ideas with us. As we continue to develop new ways to use gourmet grains, additional sections will be written for you to add to this cookbook. I am looking forward to hearing from you. Bon Appetit!

Welcome to the Mill Kitchens. We have tried all of the recipes in this book and have put together a collection of food ideas that you'll enjoy.

Gourmet cooking is both an attitude and a way of preparing and presenting food . . . it isn't a fancy name. Each of these gourmet recipes is given a name that best describes the product when it is ready to serve. Each of the recipes in this book contains a product that comes from the Stone-Buhr Mill.

The wide variety of Stone-Buhr grain products contain no chemical preservatives. Many of the Stone-Buhr products

Charlene S. Martinsen

director, Stone-Buhr Kitchens

CONTENTS

Grains have played an important role in the civilization of man. Ancient man discovered that he had more time if he cultivated grains and did not rely heavily on hunting for his food supply. Thus grain helped to change man from roving bands of people to organized communities. Ancient man ate the raw whole kernels of grain. Grains were then eaten as porridge until various forms of bread were invented. Unleavened breads such as Jewish matzos and Scotch oatcake, which people still eat today, were developed first. The Greeks, Egyptians and Romans helped to develop bread as we know it now.

We consume many grain products in the form of bread. Breads are becoming more varied as technology progresses. Producers of bread, such as Oroweat Bakers, make breads with the same wholesome quality as breads we bake at home. Bread is made from crushed grain. The story of how grain is crushed is the story of milling.

Milling began when man first crushed grain with his teeth. Next he discovered how to rub two rocks together to crush the outer husk of the seed. Each generation observed the work of grinding grain and slowly mills evolved from the first saddlestones to the millstone.

The Vitruvian mill is the true ancestor of millstones like those at Stone-Buhr. Millstones changed the grinding of grain from being a craft to a form of machine production.

GRAIN

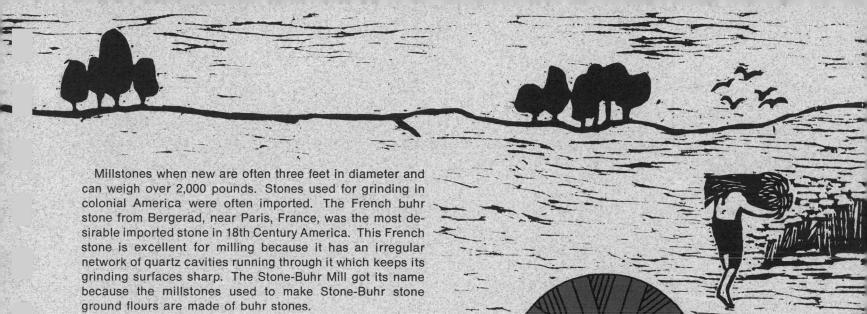

Millstones when new are often three feet in diameter and can weigh over 2,000 pounds. Stones used for grinding in colonial America were often imported. The French buhr stone from Bergerad, near Paris, France, was the most desirable imported stone in 18th Century America. This French stone is excellent for milling because it has an irregular network of quartz cavities running through it which keeps its grinding surfaces sharp. The Stone-Buhr Mill got its name because the millstones used to make Stone-Buhr stone ground flours are made of buhr stones.

The understone in a pair of millstones is set in position on a strong timber frame. The runner stone, or top stone, is balanced over the bottom stone. How close the stones are together determines how fine the grain will be milled. The flat surfaces of the grinding stones have fine grooves in them. The condition of the grooves in the stone is carefully watched. Periodically the millstones at Stone-Buhr are taken apart and the surfaces of the stone sharpened. The grooves make the grain as fine a powder as possible without overheating or subjecting the grain to undue pressure. Besides cutting the grain, the grooves also help to ventilate the surface and thus keep the flour cool. This traditional way of milling flour still goes on. Stone-Buhr 100% stone ground whole wheat flour is an example of a high quality product milled by buhr stones at the Mill.

The drawing above shows the grooving pattern of one of the millstones at Stone-Buhr. This millstone, made of buhr stone, is used to crush the hard red wheat that is used to make Stone-Buhr whole wheat flour.

FOOD STORAGE

Foods vary in the degree of temperature and the amount of moisture needed to retain quality in storage. Foods held too long or under poor storage conditions spoil.

yeast breads Breads store best in their original wrapper. Bread stays fresh longer at room temperature than in the refrigerator. In hot, humid weather, however, bread is better protected against mold stored in the refrigerator. If you do not plan to use all of the loaf of bread in 4 days, freeze half of it until you need it. Yeast dough can be frozen, unbaked, for about one week. To use it, thaw it out, shape it and allow dough to rise until doubled before baking. If possible, it is better to bake the yeast breads and then freeze them after they are cool.

Breads can be stored in the freezer for 3 months if wrapped and sealed. Thaw in the package at room temperature for about 3 hours before using. To serve hot yeast rolls or breads for breakfast, take frozen prepared rolls out of the freezer before you go to bed. In the morning, place the rolls or bread in a brown paper bag and thoroughly wet the bag. Place in a 400 degree oven for about 15 minutes or until bread is heated through. If bag starts to get too brown, sprinkle it with water again.

quick breads and cakes To store these products for short periods of time, place in closed containers and keep at room temperature. Cakes that are frosted should have the cut surface covered with plastic wrap and the rest of the cake uncovered or the frosting may become very soft and wet as the cake dries out. Cakes can be baked and then frozen for several months. Thaw in the package at room temperature for 2 hours. Many spices lose their fresh taste when a cake is frozen.

cookies Crisp cookies and soft cookies should be stored separately. Crisp cookies keep best at room temperature in a container with a loose fitting lid. Soft cookies keep best in a tightly closed container. Cookies can be baked and then frozen. To defrost, thaw in the package at room temperature. Unbaked cookie dough for rolled or drop cookies can be frozen in a freezer container for 6 months. Thaw in the package at room temperature until the dough is soft enough to shape. Bake the cookies as you normally would.

pies Fruit pies keep for only a day or two—for longer storage, it is best to freeze them. To thaw frozen pies, remove wrapped pie and allow to stand at room temperature for 3 hours, or wrap frozen pie in heavy aluminum foil and bake at 350 degrees for about 1 hour.

cereals Stone-Buhr cereal products contain no chemical

preservatives so care should be taken in storage. All of the Stone-Buhr cereal products should be stored at room temperature, in tightly closed containers that keep out dust, moisture and insects. During the summer months it is best to buy flours and cereals in small quantities. Wheat germ, however, because it has a higher proportion of fat, will stay fresher if stored in the refrigerator or freezer.

meats, poultry and fish Meat and fish are highly perishable. They should be stored in the coldest part of the refrigerator. To hold fish, poultry or ground meat for longer than 2 days, they should be frozen. Roasts, steaks and chops will stay fresh at refrigerator temperatures for 3 to 4 days. Loosening the wrappings on fresh meats slightly dries out the surface of the meat. This cuts down on bacterial spoilage and the keeping quality of the meat is better.

eggs Eggs should be refrigerated. Store in the original carton or a covered container. Storing them in the door of a refrigerator generally results in eggs that become old faster because they lose moisture through their porous shell.

butter and margarine Butter and margarine keep best at refrigerator temperatures. When allowed to stand for a long time at room temperature they take on a stale, rancid taste. Light makes butter or margarine get rancid faster, so if you really prefer to keep these spreads at room temperature be sure to keep them in a butter dish that keeps out light.

fruits Store ripe fruits uncovered in the refrigerator. When unripe, allow to ripen in the open air until ready to eat. Bananas should be stored at room temperature. Refrigerating bananas makes the peel turn brown but if eaten within a few days the fruit is still good. Dried fruits can be stored at room temperature in tightly closed containers. In warm humid weather, however, they should be refrigerated.

vegetables Vegetables stay crisper and fresher if they are in a vegetable crisper or a closed container in the refrigerator. To crisp up soggy celery and carrots, place them in icy water.

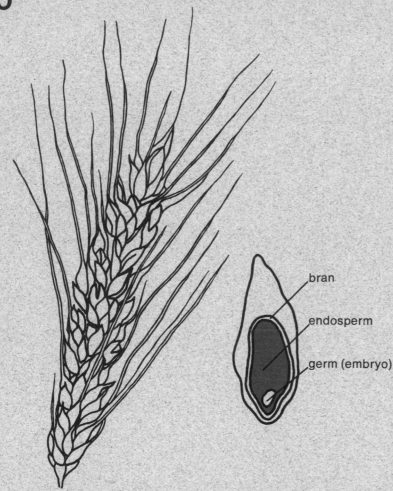

bran

endosperm

germ (embryo)

STONE-BUHR GRAINS

The grain you see on the left is a seed. The germ or embryo is the beginning of a new plant and will start to grow when the conditions are right. The endosperm contains mainly starch and protein. It is a temporary food supply for the young plant. The bran forms a covering around the seed and protects it. The bran and germ contains most of the fat, minerals, vitamins and protein in the seed. The endosperm is mainly starch.

BARLEY

Barley is one of the oldest known grains. It is cultivated in nearly every country in the world. Barley is used in preparation of malt for making beer and ale, as well as being a staple grain in many areas of northern Africa, Asia and Europe. When the husk or chaff clings tightly to the grain, special types of milling are necessary to remove them. Extracts of malt barley are used for flavoring cereals, malted milks and other food products, as barley is one of the most flavorful cereal grains. Some of the more common barley products include the following:

Barley Flakes are whole barley grains that are rolled (much the same as oats are rolled for oatmeal.)

Barley Flour is ground barley that has been hulled; however, it is not suitable for breadmaking unless used with a large proportion of wheat flour. It is suitable for certain types of pastry and other baked products and can also be used to thicken soups and gravies. (See the recipe listings under the Product Index in this book.) It may be used in small portions with other flours to add interest and appeal. To try it in recipes that you already use, start out by substituting 2 tablespoons of barley flour for 2 tablespoons of wheat flour in each cup of flour.

Pearl Barley is rounded grains of barley which have had the husks removed by coarse grinding. This is the most common form of barley used for cooking in America.

BUCKWHEAT

Buckwheat is often mistakenly called a cereal grain or grass. It belongs to the same family of plants as sorrel. The fruit of the buckwheat plant has tough brown rings surrounding the kernels and is triangular in shape. Most buckwheat is grown and consumed in Russia.

Buckwheat Flour is milled much the same way as wheat flour. Coarse sieves are used, allowing small particles of brown husks to pass through to the flour, giving it a speckled appearance. To add buckwheat flavor to recipes you now use, try substituting 2 tablespoons of buckwheat flour for 2 tablespoons of all purpose flour for each cup of all purpose flour in the recipe.

CORN

Corn is an American grain and is the principle cereal of the people in Mexico and Central America. The United States produces most of the world's corn. Corn is also used in our country in the manufacture of cereal breakfast foods, hominy, corn oil, corn syrup, cornstarch and corn whiskeys. Sweet corn is used largely as a garden vegetable. Popcorn is also a part of American tradition, particularly on festive and social occasions in the winter season.

Cornmeal is ground corn and is made from mature white or yellow corn. Cornmeal does not contain gluten and therefore cannot be used alone for making most breads. Small amounts can be added to bread recipes for added texture. It can be sprinkled generously on the bottom of pans used to bake bread. This gives the outside added "crunch."

MILLET

Millet probably originated in tropical Africa or Arabia and has been cultivated in the old world since very remote times. The Spaniards are responsible for its introduction to the new world. There are several varieties of millet, all of which belong to the grass family of plants. Millet is the chief cereal in parts of Africa and India and occupies about 20 per cent of the cultivated land of China. The grain is generally boiled or steamed, made into porridge or flour. Kasha, a porridge eaten in Russia, is made of millet and other grains, usually buckwheat and barley.

OATS

Intensive cultivation of oats is believed to have begun in

central Europe. Although it is one of the principle grain crops of Great Britain, the United States is by far the largest world producer. Oats are hulled and then rolled or cut. Only the plump grains of the annual oat crop are made into breakfast cereals. Oats have the highest protein content of any cereal grains.

Oat Flour is made from grain hulled oats that are stone ground and finely milled. It can be combined with wheat flour for added flavor in a favorite recipe. To substitute oat flour in a recipe you now use, start by replacing only 1 tablespoon of wheat flour with oat flour. Keep increasing the amount of oat flour as long as the results are satisfactory, the amount that can be used varies with each recipe.

Scotch Oatmeal is prepared from hulled oats. The grains are sliced and then slightly crushed to give a product that has some oat flour and some pieces of the grain.

Scotch Oats are made from natural, unrefined oat groats that are sliced "Scotch style" into pieces. Because of the size of the pieces, this product gives a new texture to baked products.

Old Fashioned Rolled Oats, or oatmeal, are made from whole oat groats that are softened by steam and then crushed between rollers to make rolled oats.

Quick Cooking Rolled Oats differ from old fashioned oats in that the flakes of oats are smaller than whole oats,

and can therefore cook faster.

POTATO STARCH

Potato Starch is the starch portion of potatoes. It is excellent in breadings and in baked products that have beaten egg whites as a base. Use potato starch as you would use flour, except, you must use slightly less potato starch than flour. The thickened sauce is clearer than that thickened with all-purpose flour.

RICE

Rice has been used for food since ancient times. It was introduced to America in 1686 via a ship from Madagascar which landed in Charleston, South Carolina for repairs. To show his appreciation for the hospitality of the settlers the captain presented Charleston's first settler, Henry Woodward, with a bag of rice. Much of the rice in the world is grown and consumed in Asia because it is a high yielding crop. Rice takes little fuel for preparation, which is important in the Orient where fuel is scarce and the population is crowded. Brown rice is the whole grain rice from which only the hull and a small amount of the bran has been removed. Because it has not been polished, it retains more natural salts, vitamins and minerals and has a nut-like flavor.

Brown Rice, Short Grain When short or medium grained rice is cooked, the grains are moist and tend to cling to one another. It is only one and one-half to two times as long as its width.

Brown Rice, Long Grain retains Its shape well, as It swells and generally absorbs more water than short grain. When cooked, long grain rice is light and fluffy, the grains being separate and distinct. Its length is four to five times its width.

Brown Rice Flour is made by finely grinding brown rice. Acceptable breads can be made from brown rice flour, and it is therefore very useful to people allergic to wheat. See the recipes in this book using rice flour.

White Rice Flour is made by finely grinding polished rice and may be used in the same ways as brown rice flour. To substitute rice flour in a recipe you now use, start by replacing 2 tablespoons of wheat flour with rice flour per cup of flour used. Keep increasing the amount of rice flour as long as the results are satisfactory. Brown rice flour gives more texture to products than white rice flour.

Rice Flakes are made from rice that has been rolled to form flakes similar to oatmeal. They are very crunchy and are good in cookies and toppings.

RYE

Rye, like barley, is a hardy grain crop and grows well in cooler climates. It is the principle grain bread of Germany, Russia and Scandinavian countries. Most of the rye bread made in the United States has a good portion of wheat flour mixed with it. Start out substituting only ¼ cup rye flour for ¼ cup wheat flour per cup of flour. You may continue increasing the proportion of rye as long as the product is still acceptable.

Dark Rye Flour is the flour milled from whole rye which contains all of the grain.

Rye Flakes are made from rye that is rolled to form flakes similar to oatmeal.

SOY BEANS

Soy Beans are a very nutritive, easy-cooking and economical cereal. They provide an inexpensive source of protein of high quality, oil, minerals, and practically all known vitamins. They can be served in a variety of ways—soups, casseroles, baked goods and as a natural bean vegetable.

Soy Flour is whole raw soy beans ground into flour. This flour has a slightly sweet flavor, giving smoothness and richness to products in which it is used. Replace 2 tablespoons soy flour for 2 tablespoons of wheat flour for each cup of wheat flour used.

SUNFLOWER SEEDS

Sunflower Seeds are meats from hulled large sunflowers. They are good as appetizers, as is, or they can be oiled, salted and toasted. Sunflower seeds are an excellent addition to cereals, cookies, salads, and as a nut substitute.

WHEAT

Wheat is the most widely distributed of all the cereal grains consumed. The special types of proteins in wheat form gluten which is the substance that gives the soft springy quality to bread doughs when they are being kneaded. This elastic property enables the doughs to retain the gases produced by yeast fermentation. Because of this, wheat flours can be made into soft, light, finely textured loaves of bread. Flours made from other grains do not have this type of protein and only rather heavy, solid loaves of bread can be made from them. Wheat can be grown under a wide variety of conditions, although the best growing areas are in the temperate zones where rainfall is from 13 to 35 inches per year.

All-Purpose Ernriched Wheat Flour is made from refined wheat to which certain vitamins and minerals have been added according to law. It is prepared by milling and sifting cleaned wheat. The flour consists essentially of the endosperm or inner portion of the grain. Stone-Buhr all-purpose flour is made from premium high protein spring wheat with no bleaching chemicals used. This makes a flour strong enough to make good yeast breads and fine enough for pastry, biscuits and cakes.

Gluten Flour is made from the wheat grain. The flour is washed of most starch. After drying and regrinding, the powder is concentrated high protein (41%) gluten. When using gluten flour, more soya, rye or other specialty flours can be used in baking.

Graham Flour is stone ground whole wheat flour that is coarsely milled and adds more texture to the products in which it is used. It contains all of the wheat berry.

Pastry Flour is milled from soft wheat and has a low amount of gluten potential. Its baking quality is different from cake and all-purpose flour because of this factor. It is used for soft textured cakes, pastries and for thickening liquids.

Whole Wheat Flour contains all the wheat in natural proportions, and is high in nutrients. The baking strength is less than that of white flour, consequently the volume of an all whole wheat loaf of bread will not be as great as one made with all white flour. All Stone-Buhr whole wheat flour is 100 per cent stone ground, and includes the entire wheat berry. Stone ground whole wheat flour is preferred over regularly milled wheat flour because of its richer flavor. Because whole wheat flour contains wheat germ, flour that is stored in the refrigerator or freezer will stay fresher.

Whole Wheat Pastry Flour contains whole wheat in its natural proportions, but is milled finer than regular stone ground whole wheat.

OTHER

Bran Flakes are made from the skin of wheat taken from the first breaks of the rolling process. Bran flakes can be used to add interest to toppings on desserts, as well as breading mixtures.

Cracked Wheat is prepared by cracking or cutting cleaned wheat into angular fragments.

Farina is made by grinding and sifting the wheat to a granular form. It is mainly the endosperm of the wheat grain with the bran and most of the germ removed.

Golden Farina is a combination cereal of farina, bran and rolled wheat germ.

Whole Wheat Farina is a stone ground product made from whole wheat grains that are cracked and filtered through two screens until proper fineness of the cereal is obtained.

Wheat Germ is that portion of the wheat which germinates when the kernel is planted, hence the name wheat germ. It is one of the richest sources of B and E vitamins, and also possesses valuable proteins, iron and fat. In all, it contains 30 nutrients which nature has provided for good health. After opening, it should be refrigerated, as it is perishable. Wheat germ can be added to practically all foods.

Wheat Flakes are made from whole wheat which is steamed and rolled to form flakes. Since the flakes are of the entire wheat, they make an excellent cereal or ingredient for breads.

Cereal Mates is a mixture of cut or cracked grains that are then rolled so that they are quick cooking. The equal amounts of four grains (wheat, oats, rye and barley) are used. Cereal Mates are delicious as a cooked cereal or can be used as an ingredient in almost any baked product. Cereal Mates can be used interchangeably in recipes that use oatmeal.

7 Grain Cereal is a mixture of cut or cracked wheat, oats and rye, together with bran flakes, coarsely ground corn, and a small amount of whole flax and psyllium seeds. Seven grain cereal is a delicious quick cooking hot cereal. It can also be used as an ingredient in many baked products. To use it in recipes you now use, substitute 1 tablespoon of 7 grain cereal for 1 tablespoon of flour for each cup of flour in the recipe.

ALLERGY RECIPES

This book contains some allergy recipes that are coded with the 'a' symbol above. When a person negatively reacts to a perfectly good food which most people enjoy, we say he is allergic or hypersensitive to that food. The most common food allergies are to wheat, eggs and milk. It is easy to find main dishes and vegetables that do not use these products. However, many staple foods in our diet, such as breads and desserts, include these ingredients. Only recipes which traditionally use wheat, eggs or milk but have been substituted with alternate foods are coded as allergy recipes in this book. (Refer to the Allergy index). Stone-Buhr offers a variety of grain flours that can be substituted in recipes. Preparing your own baked goods is helpful to the allergic person, as often the labels on prepared foods are not clear.

Try the recipes in this book first before trying to substitute Stone-Buhr specialty flours in your favorite standard recipes. This will give you some experience with the particular techniques that make the use of specialty flours easier. Recipes made with specialty flours are different from traditional recipes made with wheat flour. Wheat proteins form a complex network, called gluten, that give baked products their structure. Other flours do not form this network so these products are more compact. While many of the allergy recipes are not as desirable as the same recipe with wheat, milk or eggs, they are tasty and provide an opportunity for the hypersensitive individual to enjoy breads and desserts.

Rye breads often contain no milk or eggs. Gravies and sauces can be thickened with other flours besides wheat flour. See the 'Thicken Me' chart in the Vegetable Salad section. To thicken a sauce using Stone-Buhr potato starch, use about one-half as much as you would use of all-purpose flour. Rice flour thickens nicely and adds texture to the gravy. Barley flour is nice to use with beef as it contributes some of its own flavor to the gravy. Stone-Buhr oat flour is not as satisfactory for thickening gravies as oat flour contains less starch than other flours.

When you are looking for recipes that exclude milk, be sure that they do not contain butter or margarine as both of these products contain milk solids. In general, you may substitute a solid shortening in products using butter or margarine without altering the final product. Vegetable oil may be used in recipes that call for melted shortening.

MORNING GRAINS

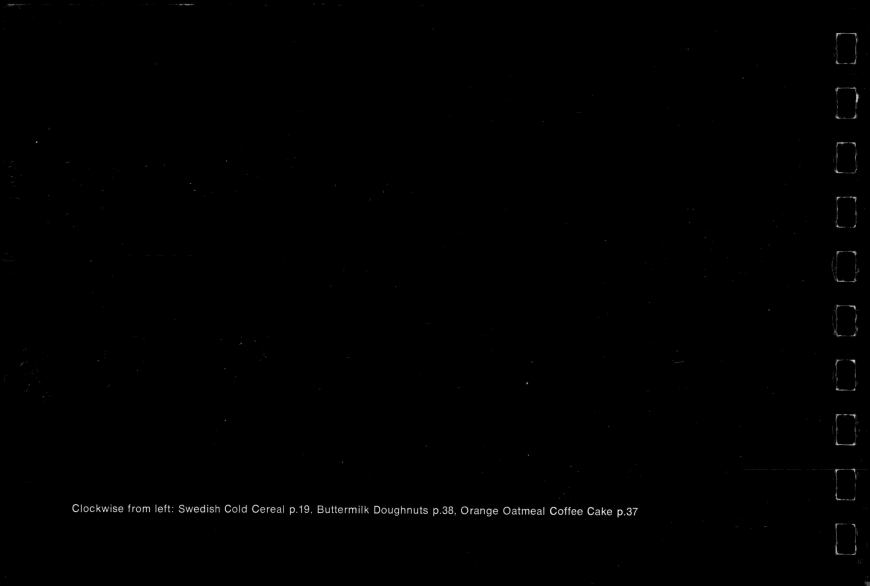

Clockwise from left: Swedish Cold Cereal p.19, Buttermilk Doughnuts p.38, Orange Oatmeal Coffee Cake p.37

CEREAL COOKING INSTRUCTIONS

Hot cereal is a traditional way to begin the day. With many varieties of grains available, an interesting variety can be served to your family. Hot cereals are especially nice during the fall and winter, because the chilly weather seems to ask for a warm way to start the day. Old fashioned cooked cereals were a mainstay of the Early American diet. Their wholesomeness and easy storage characteristics make them more desirable than many cold cereals available in the market. Hot cereal is fun to take on camping trips. It is easy to carry and tastes delicious with hot coffee, bacon and an early morning campfire. Each cereal product gives a different amount of cooked cereal. This listing will tell you how much cereal you will get from each cup of uncooked cereal. In general, most people eat about ¾ cup of cooked cereal for breakfast.

Quick Cooking Rolled Oats Bring 3 cups water and ½ tsp salt to a boil. Add 1½ cups Quick Cooking Rolled Oats and reduce heat. Cover and cook for 8 minutes, stirring occasionally. Makes 2 cups.

Old Fashioned Rolled Oats Bring 3 cups water and ½ tsp salt to a boil. Add 1 cup Old Fashioned Rolled Oats and reduce heat. Cover and cook for 20 minutes, stirring occasionally. Remove from heat and let stand covered for 2 minutes. Makes 2½ cups.

Scotch Oats and Scotch Oatmeal Bring 4 cups water and ¼ tsp salt to a boil. Add 1 cup Scotch Oats and reduce heat. Cover and cook for 25 minutes, stirring occasionally. Remove from heat and let stand covered for two minutes. Makes 3 cups.

Farina Bring 4 cups water and ½ tsp salt to a boil. Add 1 cup Farina, stirring rapidly. Reduce heat and cook for 3 minutes, stirring constantly. Makes 4 cups.

Golden Farina Stir 1 cup Farina into 4 cups of boiling water. Add ¼ tsp salt. Reduce heat. Cook, stirring constantly for 2 to 3 minutes. Makes 4 cups.

Whole Wheat Farina Bring 3 cups of water and ¼ tsp salt to a boil. Add 1 cup Whole Wheat Farina and reduce heat. Cover and cook for 5 minutes, stirring occasionally. Remove from heat and let stand for 3 minutes before eating. Makes 4 cups.

Four Grain Cereal Mates Stir 1 cup Four Grain Cereal Mates into 2 cups rapidly boiling water. Reduce heat. Cook, stirring occasionally for 7 to 8 minutes. Salt to taste. Makes 2 cups.

Seven Grain Cereal In a covered pan bring 3 cups water and ½ tsp salt to a boil. Add 1 cup Seven Grain Cereal and cook slowly until tender, about 10 minutes. Remove from heat and let stand for 5 minutes. Makes 2½ cups.

Wheat Flakes Stir 1 cup quick cooking Wheat Flakes into 2 cups rapidly boiling water. Salt to taste. Reduce heat. Cook, stirring occasionally, for 6 to 7 minutes. Makes 1½ cups.

Barley Flakes Stir 1 cup Barley Flakes into a pan containing 2 cups boiling water. Reduce heat. Cook for 5 minutes. Salt to taste. Makes 2 cups.

Rye Flakes Stir 1 cup Rye Flakes into 2 cups rapidly boiling water. Reduce heat. Cook, stirring occasionally, 15 to 18 minutes. Salt to taste. Makes 2 cups.

Rice Flakes Stir 1 cup Rice Flakes into 2 cups rapidly boiling water. Reduce heat. Cook 3 to 4 minutes. Salt to taste. Makes 2 cups.

Cracked Wheat Stir 1 cup Cracked Wheat into 3 cups rapidly boiling water. Add ¼ tsp salt. Reduce heat. Cook, stirring occasionally for 8 to 9 minutes. Makes 3½ cups.

Wheat Kernels In a covered pan, bring 5½ cups of water and ½ tsp salt to a boil. Add 1 cup Wheat Kernels, cover and cook over low heat until tender, about 2½ hours. Makes 3 cups.
Alternate method:
Soak 1 cup of Wheat Kernels in 2 cups of water overnight. Add 2 cups of water and ½ tsp of salt. Bring to a boil and cook over low heat until tender, about 1½ hours. Makes 3 cups.

SWEDISH COLD CEREAL

2   c Stone-Buhr oatmeal
1   c Stone-Buhr cereal mates
½   c Stone-Buhr wheat germ
¼   c Stone-Buhr sesame seeds
1   c coconut
1   c chopped or sliced almonds
½   c brown sugar
2   tsp vanilla
1   c light raisins
1   c chopped dried apples (optional)

This cereal is one that I adore. The toasted cereals, fruits, and nuts are a delightful combination. I think if you try it you'll make it again and again.

Mix together all the ingredients except the raisins and dried apples. Place in a large pan in a 275 degree oven for 30 minutes. Then stir well and add the dried apples. Let cereal toast for 30 more minutes, stirring well every 10 minutes. Remove from oven, add raisins and cool. Store in tightly covered containers in the refrigerator. To serve, top with milk or cream. If you prefer a cereal that is less sweet, you may decrease the amount of brown sugar. Makes 7 cups of cereal.

HOT WHEAT CEREAL

1   c Stone-Buhr wheat kernels
4 to 7   c water
½   c milk
¼   c sugar

This is a different way to serve a hot cooked cereal. You can cook the wheat a day ahead and refrigerate it. Then the next morning add the milk and finish the recipe.

In a heavy 3 to 4 quart saucepan, combine wheat kernels and 4 cups of water. Bring to a boil over high heat, cover tightly, reduce the heat to low and simmer for about 2 hours, or until the grains burst open and become soft. Check the pan frequently after the first hour of cooking and stir in more water, a cup at a time, as needed. Add the milk and sugar, cover again and simmer for 20 minutes more, or until the wheat grains are very tender. Serve hot, with additional sugar, and milk or with honey and cream. Makes 6 servings.

PUFFY FRENCH TOAST

This is the best recipe for French toast in the whole world. I like to serve it with maple syrup, flavored with Grand Marinier. Once you make French toast this way, you'll never make it any other way.

Mix together all the ingredients except the bread. Dip the bread (may be cut in thirds) and fry in ½-inch of cooking oil in a large frying pan until light brown on both sides. Remove, drain, put in baking pan until all are cooked. May then be reheated in hot oven just before serving. Serve with strawberry sweet cream dip.

Strawberry Sweet Cream Dip:

Whip ½-pint whipping cream. Stir in 3 tablespoons of sugar, ½ teaspoon of vanilla, and ½ cup sliced strawberries. Garnish with strawberries. Chill until serving time.

1	c Stone-Buhr all-purpose flour
1½	tsp baking powder
½	tsp salt
1	c milk
2	eggs
8	slices Oroweat Northridge bread

Strawberry Cream Dip:
1	c whipping cream
3	tbsp sugar
½	tsp vanilla
½	c sliced strawberries

CRISP BAKED FRENCH TOAST

This is a nice recipe for French toast prepared only in the oven —that's handy when you have many people to serve for breakfast.

Combine eggs, milk, salt and vanilla in shallow dish or pan. Dip bread in egg mixture, turning once and allowing time for both sides to absorb liquid. Coat evenly with bran flakes and place in a single layer on a well greased baking sheet. Drizzle with the margarine or butter. Bake in a 450 degree oven about 10 minutes, or until browned. Serve warm with warmed maple syrup, jelly or honey. Serves 3.

6	slices Oroweat Northridge bread
2	eggs, well beaten
½	c milk
½	tsp salt
½	tsp vanilla
1	c Stone-Buhr bran flakes
¼	c margarine or butter, melted

ⓐ OATMEAL GRIDDLE CAKES

¾ c Stone-Buhr quick oatmeal
¼ tsp baking soda
1½ c buttermilk
¾ c Stone-Buhr oat flour
1 tbsp sugar
1 tsp baking powder
½ tsp salt
1 egg
2 tbsp oil

This allergy recipe for oatmeal pancakes contains no wheat. Place bacon on a rack in a pan in a 350 degree oven for 30 minutes and you'll have a nice crisp bacon to go along with the pancakes.

Combine oatmeal, soda, buttermilk; let stand 5 minutes. Combine flour, sugar, baking powder and salt. Add dry ingredients, egg and oil to oat mixture. Stir until combined. Pour ¼ cup batter per pancake on lightly greased griddle. Makes 10.

APPLE PANCAKES

1½ c Stone-Buhr pancake mix
1 c coarsely chopped apples
½ tsp cinnamon
¾ c milk
¼ c light corn syrup
1 egg, beaten
1 tbsp butter or margarine, melted
Creamy Syrup:
¾ c maple syrup
¼ c half and half
1 tsp butter or margarine
¼ tsp vanilla

Pancakes with fruit are a pleasant change. You might also try these with fresh peaches or well-drained canned fruit cocktail.

Combine pancake mix, apples and cinnamon. Stir in remaining ingredients. Bake on hot greased griddle until bubbles break on surface. Turn and bake until golden brown. To prepare syrup: Combine maple syrup, half and half, and butter in saucepan, cook to boiling. Remove from heat; add vanilla. Serves 4.

HAWAIIAN PANCAKES

Hawaiian pancakes are nice for a summer brunch. Serve them with tall glasses of iced tea and pork sausage links.

Mix together the pancake mix, milk and egg. Add the toasted coconut and the crushed pineapple and stir well. Bake the pancakes on a hot griddle, turning once. Serves 3.

1	c Stone-Buhr pancake mix
1¼	c milk
1	egg
½	c toasted coconut
½	c crushed pineapple, drained

CORNMEAL PANCAKES

If you like cornbread, this will be a breakfast favorite. To make fresh milk sour, add about 1 tablespoon vinegar per cup of milk.

Pour water over cornmeal, stir until thick. Add milk; beat in eggs. Sift flour, baking powder, salt and soda. Add to cornmeal mixture. Stir in salad oil. Bake on hot, ungreased griddle. Yield about 14 pancakes.

1	c boiling water
¾	c Stone-Buhr yellow cornmeal
1¼	c buttermilk or sour milk
2	eggs
1	c sifted Stone-Buhr all-purpose flour
1	tbsp baking powder
1	tsp salt
¼	tsp soda
¼	c salad oil

BUCKWHEAT PECAN PANCAKES

A delicious way to serve buckwheats! These have a rich nut-like taste. Substitute sunflower seeds for pecans if you'd like.

Beat the eggs with an electric mixer until soft peaks form. Add the milk, pancake mix, sugar, oil and pecans. Stir gently until just blended. Pour onto lightly greased griddle, turn when bubbles appear. Serve with butter and syrup. Serve 3-4.

2	eggs
1	c milk
1	c Stone-Buhr buckwheat pancake mix
2	tbsp sugar
¼	c oil
¾	c coarsely chopped pecans

SESAME WHOLE WHEAT PANCAKES

1   c Stone-Buhr whole wheat
      pancake mix
1¼   c milk
1   egg
⅓   c toasted Stone-Buhr sesame seeds

Whole wheat pancakes are a nutritious breakfast treat. Serve them with griddled Canadian bacon.

Mix the pancake mix, milk and egg together. Pour about ¼ c batter for each pancake onto a lightly greased griddle. Immediately sprinkle each pancake with about 2 tsp toasted sesame seeds. Turn pancakes when bubbles appear. Serve with butter and syrup. Serves 3.

BUTTERMILK PANCAKES

2   c Stone-Buhr all-purpose flour
1   tsp baking soda
1   tsp salt
3   tbsp sugar
2   eggs
2   c buttermilk
2+   tsp oil
¼   c Stone-Buhr 7 grain cereal (optional)

Buttermilk pancakes can be varied in a number of ways. Try using banana slices or fresh blueberries instead of 7 grain cereal.

Combine flour, baking soda, salt and sugar in a bowl. Stir together to mix. Combine eggs, buttermilk and oil. Stir into flour mixture just until the flour is moistened. The batter will be a little lumpy. Place about ¼ cup batter for each pancake on a lightly greased skillet. Sprinkle top with about 2 tsp of 7 grain cereal. Turn pancakes over when bubbles appear and break around edges. Heat until browned on other side. Serve hot with whipped butter. Makes about 18 pancakes.

INDIAN PANCAKES

1   c Stone-Buhr whole wheat and soy
      pancake mix
1   c milk
1   egg
1   c creamed corn
2   tbsp sugar
4   slices of cooked bacon, crumbled

These pancakes combine the flavors of corn, wheat and bacon. They are delicious served with butter and syrup or topped with creamed tuna.

Mix pancake mix, milk, egg, creamed corn and sugar together. Add a little more milk if batter is too thick. Add bacon pieces and stir to combine. Bake pancakes on a hot griddle. Turn them once when bubbles appear over the surface of the pancake. Serves 4.

WESTERN NUGGET PANCAKES ⊚

These pancakes have a nutlike texture with cracked wheat in them. I like pineapple syrup with them.

Soak cracked wheat in 1¼ cups water for 2 hours or overnight. Stir the soaked cracked wheat with water, flour, salt, baking powder, dry milk and sugar together. Add oil or melted butter and 1 cup water; stir only until batter is smooth. Drop by spoonfuls onto a hot greased griddle. Cook slowly until pancake is covered with bubbles; turn and cook until the bottom is well browned. Makes about 20, 4-inch pancakes. Batter can be kept covered overnight in refrigerator.

1	c Stone-Buhr cracked wheat
1¼	c water
2	c Stone-Buhr all-purpose flour
2	tsp salt
1	tbsp baking powder
2	tbsp dry milk powder
2	tbsp sugar
¼	c oil, melted butter, or margarine
1	c water

COTTAGE CHEESE PANCAKES BRITTANY

These pancakes are light and moist. Serve them as soon as they are off the griddle.

Beat the eggs with sugar and salt. Add sieved cottage cheese and milk and beat well. Gradually add flour and beat until smooth. Stir in melted butter. Pour spoonfuls on greased griddle or pan. Turn when lightly browned and brown on other side. Turn only once. Serve with hot syrup. Makes 12 pancakes.

3	eggs
¼	c sugar
¼	tsp salt
1	c sieved cottage cheese
¼	c milk
1	c Stone-Buhr all-purpose or whole wheat flour
2	tbsp melted butter or margarine

BUCKWHEAT WAFFLES

1½   c Stone-Buhr whole wheat flour
¼   c Stone-Buhr buckwheat flour
¼   c Stone-Buhr wheat germ
½   tsp salt
2   tsp baking powder
1   tbsp brown sugar
4   eggs
1⅓   c milk
¼   c oil, melted butter or margarine

An old favorite. Serve with lots of whipped butter and warm syrup.

Thoroughly combine whole wheat flour, buckwheat flour, wheat germ, baking powder, brown sugar and salt in large mixing bowl. Beat eggs and stir into flour mixture. Add milk gradually, beating until batter is smooth. Stir in melted butter or oil. Bake in hot waffle iron 3 to 5 minutes. Yield 4 large waffles.

GRAHAM WAFFLES

1   c Stone-Buhr all-purpose flour, unsifted
1   c Stone-Buhr graham flour
1   tsp soda
½   tsp salt
1   tbsp sugar
2   c buttermilk
2   eggs
¼   c (⅛ lb) butter or margarine, melted

These waffles are good for breakfast or dinner. Because they have a nice crisp texture, they are especially good topped with creamed chicken.

In a large bowl, stir together flour, graham flour, soda, salt and sugar. Stir in buttermilk until blended; beat in eggs and then butter. Bake until crisp and deep golden brown in a waffle iron, following manufacturer's directions. Makes 3 large waffles (about 9 x 9 inches).

All-Graham Flour Waffles: Follow the recipe above except use 2 cups graham flour instead of the combination of flours, and increase buttermilk to 2½ cups.

CHEESE BRAN WAFFLES

If the batter gets a little too thick, add an extra tablespoon of milk.

Sift flour, baking powder and salt. Stir in bran flakes and cheese. Add egg yolks, milk and shortening to flour mixture. Beat until smooth. Beat egg whites until stiff but not dry. Fold into batter. Bake in hot waffle iron. Serve with butter and syrup or honey. Makes 4-6 large waffles.

2	c sifted Stone-Buhr all-purpose flour
1	tbsp baking powder
1	tsp salt
¾	c Stone-Buhr bran flakes
¾	c shredded sharp Cheddar cheese
2	eggs, separated
1½	c milk
¼	c melted shortening

BROWN RICE WAFFLES

These waffles are nice and crispy. Made without wheat flour they are a special treat to persons with an allergy to wheat.

Combine egg yolks, oil and milk. Mix dry ingredients together and slowly add to liquid ingredients. Fold in stiffly beaten egg whites. Bake in hot waffle iron. Makes 4 waffles.

2	c Stone-Buhr brown rice flour
1	tbsp baking powder
2	tbsp brown sugar
½	tsp salt
1¼	c milk
2	eggs, separated
6	tbsp oil

hint: Perfect waffles are easy if you remember a few pointers. ■ Preheat the waffle iron to the right temperature, beads of water will skid when it is hot. This creates a nice crisp crust. ■ Open the grids only when you are reasonably sure that they are done. This will keep the waffle from falling apart and flattening. ■ Stir waffle batter just enough to mix—overmixing makes tough waffles. ■ Clean a waffle iron with a clean stiff brush, do not wash with water and detergents. Follow manufacturers directions for greasing the irons.

WHEAT GERM WAFFLES

1¾ c sifted Stone-Buhr all-purpose flour
3 tbsp sugar
2 tsp baking powder
¾ tsp salt
⅔ c Stone-Buhr wheat germ
2 c milk
⅓ c salad oil
2 eggs, separated

Waffles are always nice for breakfast or lunch. Try topping these with creamed tuna or ham.

Sift flour, sugar, baking powder and salt. Add wheat germ and stir to mix. Combine milk, salad oil and egg yolks. Beat. Add to flour mixture; beat until smooth. Beat egg whites until stiff but not dry. Fold into batter. Bake in preheated waffle iron. Makes about 5 waffles.

SUGAR 'N SPICE MUFFINS

1 c sifted Stone-Buhr all-purpose flour
¼ c sugar
2½ tsp baking powder
½ tsp salt
½ c Stone-Buhr rolled oats (quick, or old-fashioned)
½ c Stone-Buhr cereal mates or barley flakes
½ c raisins
¼ c chopped nuts
¾ c milk
¼ c melted or liquid shortening
1 egg, beaten
Topping:
2 tbsp sugar
1 tsp cinnamon

Try serving these muffins with roast pork or ham.

Sift together flour, sugar, baking powder and salt. Stir in oats, cereal mates, raisins and nuts. Combine milk, shortening and eggs; add to dry ingredients and mix only until dry ingredients are moistened. Fill greased muffin pans ½ full. For topping: combine sugar and cinnamon; sprinkle on top of muffins. Bake at 425 degrees for 15 minutes or until done. Serve piping hot with butter. Makes 12 muffins.

APPLESAUCE MUFFINS ⓐ

These muffins are a little heavy but are moist and tasty. I usually add a little freshly ground nutmeg to the batter.

Cream shortening. Add sugar gradually. Add egg and heat well. Add applesauce. Sift soy flour and all-purpose flour with baking powder, salt and cinnamon. Add dry ingredients to applesauce mixture and blend lightly. Add nuts. Fill well-greased muffin pans ⅔'s full. Bake at 375 degrees 20 to 30 minutes or until done. Makes 12 large muffins.

¼	c shortening
¼	c sugar
1	egg
1	c applesauce
½	c unsifted Stone-Buhr soy flour
1¼	c sifted Stone-Buhr all-purpose flour
1	tbsp baking powder
½	tsp salt
1	tsp cinnamon
½	c chopped nut meats

RYE MUFFINS ⓐ

This allergy recipe contains no milk, eggs or wheat. The muffins have a good flavor and a nice crunchy texture. They do not store well, so make just enough for 1 day.

Mix dry ingredients together thoroughly. Add water and fat and stir to moisten dry ingredients. Fill well-greased muffin pans ⅔'s full. Bake 25 minutes at 375 degrees or until done. Makes 10 muffins.

1¼	c unsifted Stone-Buhr rye flour
½	c unsifted Stone-Buhr rice flour
4	tsp baking powder
¾	tsp salt
¼	c sugar
1	c water
¼	c melted shortening

SOY MUFFINS

This combination of wheat and soy flours is delicious. The soy flour is high in protein and gives these muffins a golden color.

Sift flours and measure. Resift 2 times with baking powder and salt. Cream butter. Add sugar gradually creaming well. Beat in egg until fluffy. Stir in milk. Add to flour mixture all at once and stir just to dampen ingredients. Fill greased muffin pans ⅔'s full. Bake at 425 degrees for about 20 minutes or until done. Makes 10 to 12 muffins.

1½	c Stone-Buhr all-purpose flour
½	c Stone-Buhr soy flour
4	tsp baking powder
½	tsp salt
¼	c butter or margarine
¼	c sugar
1	egg
1	c milk

WHOLE WHEAT MUFFINS

1 egg
1 c milk
¼ c salad oil
1 c sifted Stone-Buhr all-purpose flour
1 c unsifted Stone-Buhr whole wheat flour
¼ c sugar
1 tbsp baking powder
1 tsp salt

Serve these muffins with butter and honey. They are delicious for breakfast or with fried chicken.

Mix egg, milk and oil together well. In a bowl, place all the dry ingredients and stir until well mixed. Make a well in center and add milk mixture. Stir just enough to moisten dry ingredients. Fill greased muffin pans ⅔'s full. Bake at 400 degrees for 20 to 25 minutes or until done. Makes 12 muffins.

POPEYE CEREAL MUFFINS

2½ c Stone-Buhr cereal mates or 7-grain cereal
2¼ c milk
½ c raisins
⅔ c soft shortening
1 egg
2 c sifted Stone-Buhr all-purpose flour
⅔ c sugar
4 tsp baking powder
1 tsp salt

You can use either the 4 or 7-grain cereal blend by Stone-Buhr for these muffins.

Combine cereal and milk. Let stand about 10 minutes and then add the raisins. Add shortening and egg; beat well. Sift together flour, sugar, baking powder and salt; add to cereal mixture. Stir only until combined. Fill greased muffin pans ¾'s full. Bake at 400 degrees for 25 to 30 minutes, or until lightly browned. Serve hot. Makes 12 medium muffins.

GOLD SURPRISE MUFFINS ⓐ

The surprise in these muffins is carrot. It makes the muffins sweet and moist. I usually add ½ cup chopped nuts also.

Beat shortenning and sugar together until creamy. Add eggs; beat until light and fluffy. Add lemon juice, water and carrots; stir until well blended. Combine remaining ingredients; add to carrot mixture and stir only until dry ingredients are moistened. Fill greased muffin pans ⅔'s full. Bake at 400 degrees for 20 minutes or until muffins start to pull away from sides of pan. Makes about 12 muffins.

¼	c shortening
¼	c brown sugar
2	eggs
1	tbsp lemon juice
1	tbsp water
1	c finely shredded carrots, lightly packed
½	c sifted Stone-Buhr all-purpose flour
½	c 7-grain cereal
2	tsp baking powder
½	tsp salt
¼	tsp ground ginger

WHEAT FREE MUFFINS ⓐ

This allergy recipe contains no wheat. I think these muffins are delightful and easy to prepare.

Combine dry ingredients; add remaining ingredients and mix enough to moisten. Bake in well greased muffin pans at 350 degrees for 20 to 30 minutes or until done. Makes 6 muffins.

¾	c unsifted Stone-Buhr rice flour
¼	c unsifted Stone-Buhr soy flour
¼	c sugar
2	tsp baking powder
¼	tsp soda
¼	tsp salt
½	c buttermilk
¼	c cottage cheese
2	tbsp melted butter or margarine
1	egg, beaten

CORN GEMS

1	c sifted Stone-Buhr all-purpose flour
3	tbsp sugar
1½	tsp baking powder
½	tsp soda
½	tsp salt
1	c Stone-Buhr yellow cornmeal
1	egg, well beaten
⅔	c buttermilk
¼	c shortening, melted

These cornmeal muffins are a favorite in southern homes in the United States. If you do not use buttermilk, leave out the soda and add an extra ½ teaspoon of baking powder.

Sift flour, sugar, baking powder, soda and salt into a large bowl; stir in cornmeal. Mix egg and buttermilk; add all at once to flour mixture; stir lightly with a fork just until liquid is absorbed; stir in melted shortening. Spoon into greased muffin pans, filling each ⅔'s full. Bake at 400 degrees for 10 to 15 minutes, or until golden; remove from pan. Serve hot. Makes 12 muffins.

BREAKFAST MUFFINS

1	c sifted Stone-Buhr all-purpose flour
1¼	tsp baking powder
1	tbsp sugar
½	tsp salt
1	egg, well beaten
⅓	c milk
¼	c melted shortening, or salad oil

Breakfast muffins are easy to prepare. This recipe makes only 6 muffins, which is just enough for one meal.

Measure sifted flour, add baking powder, sugar and salt and sift again. Combine egg and milk and add all at once to flour mixture. Add shortening, stir only until dry ingredients are dampened. (Batter will be lumpy). Spoon into greased muffin pans, filling each ⅔'s full. Bake at 400 degrees about 25 minutes or until done.

BLUEBERRY MUFFINS

1¾	c sifted Stone-Buhr all-purpose flour
¼	c sugar
2½	tsp baking powder
¾	tsp salt
1	egg
¾	c milk
⅓	c oil
1	c blueberries (well drained if canned or frozen)

Blueberry muffins are my favorite! These taste good with everything. Be sure you make enough for everyone.

Sift dry ingredients together into mixing bowl; make a well in center. Combine egg, milk, and salad oil. Add all at once to dry ingredients. Add blueberries and stir quickly only until dry ingredients are moistened. Fill greased muffin pans ⅔'s full. Bake at 400 degrees for about 25 minutes or until done. Makes about 12 muffins.

BEAR CLAWS

These rolls are delicious. One family I know always has them for breakfast on Easter Sunday.

Sprinkle yeast into warm water and let stand until dissolved. Cream the butter until light and beat in sugar. Beat in egg yolks. Then add yeast mixture, milk, salt and cardamon. Gradually mix in the flour. Dough will be quite soft. Turn out on a floured board and knead until smooth. Return dough to bowl and butter the top lightly. Cover and let rise in a warm place about 1½ hours or until doubled in bulk. Turn dough out on floured surface and knead lightly. With floured rolling pin roll half the dough out 8-inches wide, 27-inches long and ¼-inch thick.

Next make the Streusel Filling by mixing sugar, flour, butter, cocoa and cinnamon together until crumbly. Sprinkle half of the Streusel Filling evenly over the yeast dough, covering to within 1-inch of the edges. Roll up jellyroll fashion from a long side. Pinch ends to seal. Cut into 3-inch segments and shape into bear claws by slashing each piece twice. Place on greased cookie sheet. Repeat with other half of the dough. Cover and let rise in a warm place until doubled.

Bake in a 325 degree oven for 20 to 25 minutes or until richly brown. While still warm, spread top of each roll with Powdered Sugar Glaze, made by mixing the powdered sugar, milk and vanilla together. Makes 1½ dozen rolls.

Dough:
- 1 pkg yeast, active dry or compressed
- ¼ c warm water
- ½ c soft butter or margarine
- ⅓ c sugar
- 3 egg yolks
- ¾ c milk, scalded and cooled
- ¼ tsp salt
- ¼ tsp ground cardamon
- 3 c unsifted Stone-Buhr all-purpose flour

Chocolate Streusel Filling:
- ½ c sugar
- ¼ c Stone-Buhr all-purpose flour
- 2 tbsp butter or margarine
- 1½ tsp unsweetened cocoa
- ½ tsp cinnamon

Powdered Sugar Glaze:
- 4 tsp milk
- ½ tsp vanilla
- 1 c powdered sugar

WALNUT SOUR CREAM COFFEE CAKE

This coffee cake is good when eaten warm. Serve it with spiced tea.

Batter:
- 1 c butter or margarine
- 1 c sugar
- 1 tsp vanilla
- 2 eggs
- 2 c sifted Stone-Buhr all-purpose flour
- 1 tsp baking powder
- 1 tsp soda
- ½ tsp salt
- 1 c sour cream

Filling and Topping:
- ⅓ c firmly packed brown sugar
- ¼ c sugar
- 1 tsp cinnamon
- ⅔ c Stone-Buhr cereal mates
- ½ c chopped walnuts

For batter, cream butter and sugar together until light and fluffy. Blend in vanilla. Add eggs one at a time. Beat until smooth. Sift together flour, baking powder, soda and salt. Add to creamed mixture alternately with sour cream.

For filling and topping:
Combine all ingredients thoroughly. Turn half the batter into buttered 9-inch square baking pan. Sprinkle with half the brown sugar mixture. Cover with remaining batter and sprinkle with the rest of the sugar mixture. Bake at 350 degrees for 50 minutes. Yields 9 servings.

BANANA NUT COFFEE RING

For that 10 o'clock coffee break! This is a good banana bread baked in a ring.

- 1 c sugar
- 1 3-oz pkg cream cheese, softened
- 1 egg
- 1 tsp vanilla
- ¾ c chopped walnuts
- 1½ c mashed bananas
- ½ c Stone-Buhr farina
- 2 c sifted Stone-Buhr all-purpose flour
- 1 tsp baking powder
- 1 tsp soda
- ½ tsp salt
- ½ tsp cinnamon
- ½ tsp nutmeg

Cream sugar with softened cream cheese; beat in egg and vanilla. Stir in nuts and bananas. Sift together remaining ingredients. Add to banana mixture; stir just until blended. Spread evenly in greased 6½ cup ring mold. Bake in 350 degree oven 30 to 35 minutes or until done. Cool in pan 10 minutes; then turn out on wire rack to cool completely. Wrap tightly and store overnight before serving. Makes 36 ¾-inch slices.

PEACHY BREAKFAST BREAD

This is a nice bread to serve at brunch. I serve it with cold sliced meats and cheese for a German style breakfast.

Sift flour, sugar, baking powder, salt and spices. Stir in cereal mates and nuts. Combine milk, egg and ½ cup of melted butter. Stir into dry ingredients until moistened. Do not beat. Pour batter into greased 8 x 8 x 2-inch pan. Bake 375 degrees for 40 to 45 minutes or until done. Cool in pan. Chop or slice peaches. Arrange on cooled bread. Dribble 3 tablespoons of melted butter on top and sprinkle with brown sugar. Broil 4 inches from broiler unit until topping bubbles and tops of peaches begin to brown. Cut in squares. Makes 9 servings.

1¾	c sifted Stone-Buhr all-purpose flour
¾	c sugar
4½	tsp baking powder
¾	tsp salt
1½	tsp cinnamon
¾	tsp nutmeg
¼	tsp cloves
1½	c Stone-Buhr cereal mates, uncooked
½	c chopped nuts
⅔	c milk
1	egg, slightly beaten
½	c melted butter or margarine
1	can (1 lb 14 oz) cling peaches, well-drained
⅓	c brown sugar
3	tbsp melted butter or margarine

CINNAMON ORANGE COFFEE BREAD

2 c sifted Stone-Buhr all-purpose flour
1½ tsp baking powder
⅛ tsp soda
½ tsp salt
⅔ c sugar
1 tsp cinnamon
½ tsp nutmeg
½ c shortening
2 tbsp grated orange peel
⅓ c chopped nuts
1 egg
½ c milk
½ c sugar
2 tsp melted butter
½ tsp cinnamon

This coffee bread is not very sweet. It is good when spread with butter or cream cheese.

Sift flour and baking powder; add soda, salt, sugar and spices. Cut in shortening with pastry blender until mixture resembles fine crumbs. Add orange peel and nuts. Combine egg and milk. Add to flour mixture. Mix enough to moisten flour. Spread evenly in greased 9x9x2-inch pan. Sprinkle with cinnamon topping. Cinnamon topping: Combine sugar, melted butter and cinnamon. Blend to make crumbly mixture. Bake in 375 degree oven for 25 minutes.

GERMAN BLUEBERRY KUCHEN

1 c sifted Stone-Buhr all-purpose flour
½ c Stone-Buhr graham flour, unsifted
2 tsp baking powder
½ tsp salt
¾ c sugar
¼ c soft shortening
⅔ c milk
1 tsp vanilla
1 egg
1½ tsp grated lemon peel
1 c fresh blueberries
3 tbsp sugar

Blueberries and lemon peel make a good coffee cake. If you have any left, cover with foil and reheat it in a 350 degree oven for 10 minutes.

Stir together flours, baking powder, salt and ¾ cup of sugar. Add shortening, milk, vanilla and ½ teaspoon grated lemon peel. Beat with electric mixer on medium speed for 3 minutes, or 300 strokes by hand. Add egg and beat with mixer 2 minutes longer, or 200 strokes by hand. Turn into well greased 8 x 8 x 2 pan. Lightly stir together blueberries, 3 tablespoons sugar and 1 teaspoon grated lemon peel, and spoon onto batter. Bake at 350 degrees 40 to 45 minutes or until lightly browned. Cool slightly in pan. Cut into squares and serve warm. Yield 6 to 9 servings.

PECAN ROLLS

This is a new twist to pecan rolls. The delicate maple flavor makes these a real treat. You can omit the 2nd raising and refrigerate the rolls overnight. The next morning place them directly in a preheated oven.

In mixer bowl, blend 1½ c all-purpose flour, the scotch oatmeal, ½ c brown sugar, salt and dry yeast. Heat the milk and margarine add to flour mixture. Beat for 4 minutes at medium speed. By hand, stir in about 1½ c more flour to form a stiff dough. Cover and let rise until double. Grease a 9x13-inch pan. Spread in a mixture of the maple syrup, ¼ c brown sugar, ¼ c margarine and ⅔ c pecans. Punch down dough and drop spoonfulls on topping in pan. Brush the dough with melted butter and sprinkle with ½ c brown sugar and ½ tsp cinnamon. Cover and let rise until double. Bake at 350 degrees for 30 min or until lightly browned. Remove from oven and invert onto serving plate. Serves 5 to 6.

Dough:
- 3 c Stone-Buhr all-purpose flour
- 1 c Stone-Buhr scotch oatmeal
- ½ c brown sugar
- 1½ tsp salt
- 1 pkg active dry or cake yeast
- 1 c milk
- ½ c butter or margarine

Topping:
- ½ c maple syrup
- ¼ c brown sugar
- ¼ c margarine or butter
- ⅔ c pecans
- ½ c brown sugar
- ½ tsp cinnamon

ORANGE-OATMEAL COFFEE CAKE

Batter:
- ½ c butter or margarine
- 1 c sugar
- 2 eggs
- 1½ c sifted Stone-Buhr all-purpose flour
- 2 tsp baking powder
- ½ tsp cinnamon
- ¼ tsp salt
- ½ c Stone-Buhr rice flakes
- ½ c Stone-Buhr quick-cooking oatmeal, uncooked
- 1 c milk

Glaze:
- ¼ c butter or margarine
- ½ c firmly packed light brown sugar
- ½ c chopped nuts
- 3 tbsp orange juice

This coffee cake is delicious. The orange glaze is attractive and really tastes great!

In a large mixing bowl cream butter. Gradually add sugar and beat until light and fluffy. Beat in eggs one at a time. Sift together flour, baking powder, cinnamon and salt; mix in oatmeal and rice flakes. Add to creamed mixture alternately with milk beginning and ending with dry ingredients. Turn into a buttered 8-inch square pan. Bake in 350 degree oven 35 to 45 minutes. While warm, spread with Orange Glaze. To prepare Orange Glaze: In a small mixing bowl cream butter, stir in sugar, nuts and juice. Spread over cake. Place under broiler until topping is bubbly, about 2 minutes. Cool cake slightly in pan on wire rack before serving. Yield 9 servings.

GOLDEN ORANGE DOUGHNUTS

- 1½ c milk
- 1 c instant mashed potatoes
- ¼ c butter or margarine
- 1½ c Stone-Buhr whole wheat flour
- 3 c Stone-Buhr sifted all-purpose flour
- 5 tsp baking powder
- 1½ tsp salt
- 1 tsp mace
- 3 eggs
- 1⅓ c sugar
- 2 tbsp grated orange rind
- 1 tsp vanilla

Doughnuts are nice to serve with cider. Have a plateful ready for when you get home from the football game.

Scald milk; add potatoes and stir until smooth. Add butter and stir until butter is melted. Chill. Mix whole wheat flour, all-purpose flour, baking powder, salt and mace. Add eggs to potato mixture, one at a time, beating well after each addition. Add sugar, orange rind and vanilla; beat well. Add dry ingredients and blend to make soft dough. Chill well. Use a small amount of dough at a time. Roll dough to ½-inch thickness on floured board. Cut with floured 2½ inch doughnut cutter. Fry in deep hot fat, 375 degrees, about 3 minutes, until browned, turning once. Drain on paper toweling. Dip in sugar or powdered sugar, if desired. Makes 2 to 2½ dozen doughnuts.

BUTTERMILK DOUGHNUTS

I save the fat used in frying doughnuts. Strain it through cheese-cloth or a piece of paper towel to remove particles of food and store the strained fat in the original container or one with a tight lid.

Combine flour, baking powder, soda, salt and nutmeg and sift together several times. In a separate bowl combine the butter-milk (which has been standing at room temperature several hours) the melted butter or shortening, vanilla, egg and sugar. Add dry ingredients to the buttermilk mixture and beat only until dough leaves sides of bowl. Turn out onto well floured covered board and knead gently for about ½ minute, adding only enough more flour to prevent sticking. Pat and roll to about ⅓-inch in thickness if using 2½-inch cutter (¼-inch thick if using smaller cutter). Let stand about a minute to recover from shock of rolling; then cut through with doughnut cutter, dipping it into flour occasionally. Lower into deep fat that has been heated to about 365 degrees, placing doughnuts on a pancake turner when dropping into fat, as they are very soft and may break in handling. Allow doughnuts to fry on one side until golden brown and then turn over and fry second side. Remove carefully with a long skewer, a fork or a pair of tongs. Place on cake rack. When they are cool, sprinkle both sides thickly with confectioners sugar. Makes about 8 to 12 doughnuts.

2¼	c sifted Stone-Buhr all-purpose flour
1¼	tsp double-acting baking powder
½	tsp soda
½	tsp salt
½	tsp nutmeg
½	c buttermilk at room temperature
2	tbsp melted butter or other shortening
½	tsp vanilla
1	very large whole egg (room temperature) beaten
½	c granulated sugar
	Confectioners sugar

VEGETABLES & SALADS

Clockwise from left: Southern Spoon Bread p.48, Baked Beans p.46, Hot German Salad p.52, Chinese Broccoli p.40

VEGETABLES & SALADS

Salads and Vegetables put color and variety in our menus. Servings of Salads and Vegetables should vary with the season of the year.

Early spring is the time for fresh spinach and radishes. Strawberries come to the market in April and after the long winter, a fruit salad with canned fruit cocktail, fresh strawberries and bananas is a nice accompaniment to chicken grilled over charcoal. Fresh asparagus is generally available only in the spring. I always peel the bottom half of each spear using a potato peeler. Then, I tie the asparagus into a bundle using some heavy string. After cooking quickly in a tightly covered pan, I can lift the vegetable out easily and arrange it by merely removing the string. Allow about 2 pounds of asparagus for 4 generous servings.

Summer brings a variety of fresh vegetables and salad greens. Tossed salads become gourmet when you add some sliced fresh mushrooms or zucchini. Cherry tomatoes stuffed with seasoned cream cheese are easy to prepare and are a nice appetizer during warm weather. Salads can be used to perk up waning hot weather appetites. A lavish tray filled with chilled marinated vegetables, sharp cheeses and cold meats can be carried to an eating spot out of doors, whether it's the beach or on your own patio. Finding a cool spot to eat is easy when your menu is composed of fresh produce.

Winter means colder weather and a chance to prepare heartier salads and winter vegetables. Hot German salads and baked squash signal the start of the football season. Spicy German sausages are always appealing and go nicely with warm soy bean dishes. Carrots, squash, turnips, rutabaga, onions and potatoes are all available at reasonable prices. Try mashing cooked carrots or rutabaga with potatoes. The result will be a delicately flavored and softly colored dish of fluffy potatoes. All year around vegetables are available fresh, frozen or in cans. Try them all—you will be delighted with the tasty adventure of it all.

CHINESE BROCCOLI

Be sure to slice the broccoli stems thin. Do not cover the broccoli until the mixture has come to a boil. This will keep the broccoli a bright green color.

Trim outer leaves and tough ends from broccoli. Cut stalks and flowerets into 2-inch lengths, then slice thin lengthwise. Combine butter or margarine, water and soy sauce in a large frying pan; heat to boiling. Stir in broccoli, celery, and water chestnuts. Heat to boiling again; cover. Steam 5 to 10 minutes, or just until broccoli is crisply tender. While broccoli cooks, heat sesame seeds in a small heavy frying pan over low heat, shaking pan constantly, just until lightly toasted; stir into broccoli mixture. Spoon into a heated serving bowl. Serve with additional soy sauce to sprinkle over top. Makes 4 servings.

1	bunch broccoli, weighing about 1½ lbs.
¼	c (½ stick) butter or margarine
¼	c water
1	tbsp soy sauce
1	c thinly sliced celery
1	can (5 oz) water chestnuts, drained and sliced (optional)
1	tbsp Stone-Buhr sesame seeds

POTATO-CHEESE PATTIES

Use leftover mashed potatoes or make instant ones. These seasoned patties go well with any roast.

Combine first 4 ingredients and shape into patties. Dip in the crumb mixture. Place patties on greased cookie sheet and bake at 325 degrees 20 to 25 minutes or until brown. Makes 6 servings.

Potato Patties:
3	c mashed potatoes
½	c shredded cheese (packed)
1	tsp salt
¼	tsp pepper

Crumb Mixture:
½	c Stone-Buhr bran flakes
½	c Stone-Buhr wheat germ
2	tbsp dried parsley
1	tbsp onion salt

CAULIFLOWER AU GRATIN

1   10-oz pkg frozen cauliflower
Sauce:
1   tbsp butter or margarine
1   tbsp Stone-Buhr all-purpose flour
¼   tsp salt
⅛   tsp pepper
1   tsp dry mustard
1   c milk
1   c grated processed American cheese
Topping:
¼   c Stone-Buhr wheat germ
¼   c Stone-Buhr bran flakes
1   tbsp melted butter or margarine
⅛   tsp salt
¼   tsp sage
⅛   tsp dry mustard

A cheese sauce and crumb topping makes almost every vegetable taste special. Try this with left-over vegetables.

Thaw cauliflower and spread in bottom of ungreased 1 quart casserole. Prepare white sauce by melting butter in fry pan. Blend in flour and seasonings; stir until smooth. Remove from heat and stir in milk. Heat to boiling, stirring constantly. Stir in grated cheese and stir until melted. Pour over vegetable. Combine the ingredients for topping and sprinkle over the sauce. Bake uncovered for 15 minutes at 325 degrees or until vegetable is heated through and crispy tender. Green beans, broccoli or leftover vegetables may be used. Makes 4 servings.

STUFFED ACORN SQUASH

3   acorn squash, halved and seeded
1   lb pork sausage, cooked and drained
⅔   c milk
1   tsp salt
¼   tsp pepper
1   tsp dry mustard
½   c sweet pickle relish
¾   c Stone-Buhr oatmeal
2   tbsp sliced black olives
6   slices mozarella cheese
    Paprika

This is a nice combination of squash and filling. You can cook squash ahead of time, stuff them with the filling and refrigerate until you are ready to use them. Then bake for 15 minutes longer than the recipe indicates.

Heat oven to 425 degrees. Place squash cut side down in shallow baking pan. Pour a little water in pan. Bake 30 minutes. Remove from oven and turn squash cut side up. For filling, combine remaining ingredients except cheese and paprika. Spoon in squash centers. Add a little water to pan and return to oven. Reduce temperature to 350 degrees and bake 20 minutes. Remove from oven and place a slice of cheese on each half squash. Sprinkle with paprika. Return to oven for 10 minutes, or until squash is tender. Makes 6 servings.

BROCCOLI CASSEROLE

This broccoli casserole is very rich. The rice and custard base is a nice change for a vegetable dish.

Cook broccoli; drain thoroughly. Saute onion in butter; add seasonings. Mix broccoli, onion and remaining ingredients. Turn into a buttered 1½-quart casserole. Bake at 325 degrees for about 1 hour and 15 minutes or until custard is set (knife comes out clean). 8 servings.

1	pkg (10 oz) frozen chopped broccoli
½	c chopped onion
2	tbsp butter or margarine
1	tsp salt
¼	tsp pepper
2	eggs, slightly beaten
2	c milk
2	c cooked Stone-Buhr long grain brown rice
1½	c grated sharp cheese

SCALLOPED POTATOES ⊙

Potato starch helps to give these scalloped potatoes a rich, full taste.

Peel potatoes and slice them paper thin. Do the same with onions. In the bottom of a 3 quart, buttered baking dish, arrange a layer of potato slices. Sprinkle lightly with starch, season and place a few onion slices on top. Dot with butter. Continue layers in this fashion until ingredients are used up. Pour in milk to cover. (Use dish deep enough so milk is at least ¾-inch from top or it will bubble over). Sprinkle with wheat germ. Bake, covered in 325 degree oven for 1 hour. Remove cover and continue baking until top is lightly browned (about 10 minutes). Makes 6 servings.

5	medium potatoes
2	medium onions
1½	c Stone-Buhr potato starch for dredging
1	tsp salt
⅛	tsp pepper
¼	c butter or margarine
	Milk to cover (about 3 cups)
¼	c Stone-Buhr wheat germ

IN-BETWEEN BEANS

3	c dried Stone-Buhr soy beans
8	c water
¼	lb salt pork, diced
1½	c diced onion
¼	c dark molasses
2	tbsp dry mustard
2	tbsp prepared mustard
2	tbsp Worcestershire sauce
1	c beer
1	tbsp salt
¼	c brown sugar
6	drops liquid hot pepper seasoning, or to taste
1	lg can (15 oz) tomato sauce

A kind of baked beans without much tomato. These beans are better when reheated. This is a large recipe and is fun to take to a picnic.

Cover beans with the water and soak overnight (or cover with the water; bring to boil, boil 2 minutes, remove from heat, cover, and allow to soak for 1 hour). Without draining beans, place in a large (about 5 quart) baking dish. Add pork, onion, molasses, dry mustard, prepared mustard, Worcestershire sauce, beer, salt, sugar and liquid hot pepper seasoning. Bake, covered, in a 300 degree oven for 3 to 4 hours, or until beans are almost tender. Remove from oven, stir in tomato sauce; bake, uncovered, for 2 more hours or until beans are tender. Add additional water if beans get dry before they are tender. Serve as a main dish for supper or as a dinner side dish with barbecued meats. Makes 12 to 16 servings.

CORN SESAME SAUTE

1	10-oz pkg frozen corn
2	tbsp butter or margarine
1	clove garlic, crushed
2	tbsp Stone-Buhr sesame seeds
2	tbsp chopped green pepper
½	tsp salt
¼	tsp basil leaves
⅛	tsp pepper

A delicious new way to serve corn. Try substituting marjoram or savory for the basil.

Cook and stir all ingredients over medium heat until butter is melted. Cover; cook over low heat 10 minutes or until corn is tender. About 3 servings.

BRUSSELS SPROUTS
with CREAM SAUCE

Properly cooked, fresh vegetables are a delight to any meal. In the summer, fresh vegetables are a good buy. In the winter, check frozen and canned vegetables as they are often less expensive than fresh vegetables.

Trim off the stem and the discolored leaves from the brussels sprouts and cook in salted water for 15 minutes. Drain and cook uncovered in boiling salted water to cover just until tender, about 15 minutes. Meanwhile, melt the butter in a pan. Add the rye flour and salt and mix thoroughly. Add the milk and bring to a boil, stirring occasionally. Set aside over low heat until brussels sprouts are cooked. Drain brussels sprouts and place in a heated serving bowl. Pour sauce over vegetables and serve. Serves 6.

3	c fresh brussels sprouts
2	tbsp butter or margarine
2	tbsp Stone-Buhr dark rye flour
¼	tsp salt
1	c milk

The chart on the next page gives you an idea of how to use many of the specialty flours in thickening sauces and puddings. Remember that the texture will be a little different. The flavor characteristics of each grain also come through. Experiment!

THICKEN ME

sauce	flour	butter	liquid	uses
thin	1 tbsp	1 tbsp	1 c	soups, thin sauces
medium	2 tbsp	2 tbsp	1 c	gravies, puddings
thick	3 tbsp	2½ tbsp	1 c	bind things together, croquettes

Variety flours can be used daily to thicken gravies, sauces and stews. Experiment on your own, use them to dust meat or fish before browning, their added variety is great.

In sauces, substitute the following Stone-Buhr products for all-purpose flour:

Pastry flour, whole wheat flour, rice flour, rye flour, brown rice flour, barley flour or ½ as much potato starch.

kind of flour	characteristics
pastry flour	thickens like all-purpose flour
whole wheat flour	gives whole wheat flavor and is a little thinner
brown and white rice flour	gives texture to the sauce
rye flour	gives a delicious rich flavor
barley flour	gives a strong barley flavor, good in hearty meat dishes
potato starch	gives a soft, clear sauce that is thicker than flour

BAKED BEANS

Everyone loves baked beans. Prepare these for your next picnic.

Wash beans and place in water. Soak overnight or boil 2 minutes, and let stand 1 hour. Cut salt pork in pieces and add to beans. Cook for 1½ hours, or until almost tender. Add salt, onion, brown sugar, mustard and molasses. Put beans in 3 qt. baking pan. Add water if necessary to cover beans. Cover and bake at 350 degrees for 1½ to 2 hours or until tender. Makes 6-8 servings.

2	c Stone-Buhr soy beans
7	c water
¼	lb salt pork
1½	tsp salt
1	onion, chopped
¼	c brown sugar
1	tsp mustard
½	c molasses

SOY BEANS PRINTANIER

Printanier means spring vegetables such as carrots, green peppers and onions. I think this is a delicious side dish.

Saute onions, carrots, green peppers and tomatoes in oil for 15 minutes over low heat. Mix with remaining ingredients except cheese. Pour into well-greased baking dish. Top with shredded cheese, cover and bake at 325 degrees for 25 to 30 minutes. Makes 4-6 servings.

½	c chopped green onions or chives
½	c shredded carrots
½	c chopped green peppers
1½	c diced tomatoes
1	tbsp oil
2	c cooked Stone-Buhr soy beans
½	c Stone-Buhr wheat germ
1	tsp fresh sweet basil, or ¼ tsp dried basil
2	tbsp margarine
¼	c brown sugar
	Salt to taste
¾	c shredded sharp cheddar cheese

SOY BEAN CASSEROLE

1 c Stone-Buhr soy beans, soaked in water overnight
2 tbsp diced salt pork
1 c sliced celery
2 tbsp chopped onion
1 tbsp sliced green pepper
3 tbsp Stone-Buhr all-purpose flour
1 c milk
½ tsp salt
¼ c Stone-Buhr wheat germ

This is a delicious casserole. The crumb topping makes it even better. If you don't have a pressure cooker, simmer the soy beans for 1½ hrs. or until tender, using a regular pan.

Cook soy beans in pressure pan at 15 pounds pressure till tender (about 30 minutes). Brown the salt pork in a frying pan. Add the celery, onion, and green pepper, and cook for about 5 minutes or until vegetables are tender. Add the flour and mix well. Gradually add the milk and salt and stir until it reaches the boiling point. Stir in the cooked, drained beans and pour the mixture into a baking dish. Cover with wheat germ. Bake at 350 degrees for 30 minutes, or until the wheat germ is golden brown. Makes 6 servings.

SOY BEANS and MILLET CASSEROLE

1 c cooked Stone-Buhr soy beans
1 c cooked Stone-Buhr millet
½ c chopped onions or scallions
½ c chopped green pepper
¾ c chopped mushrooms
1 tsp oil
2 eggs, beaten
2 tbsp margarine
¾ c tomato juice
1 tsp fresh marjoram or sage, chopped
¼ c brown sugar
Salt to taste

Soy beans and millet are combined to make an interesting dish. Use this casserole as a substitute for potatoes or serve as a main dish.

Cook soy beans and millet according to package directions. Set aside. Saute onions, green peppers and mushrooms in oil for 10 minutes. Mix in remaining ingredients. Bake in well greased casserole at 325 degrees, about 45 to 50 minutes. Serves 4 to 6.

SOUTHERN SPOON BREAD SOUFFLE

This is really delicious. Prepare it when you have roast pork or fish and you'll have a dinner to remember.

Scald milk. Add cornmeal and cook until mixture is very thick. Add salt and baking powder. Beat egg yolks until light and add a little of the hot cornmeal mixture and then combine both mixtures. Add butter. Beat egg whites to soft peak stage and fold in. Put in buttered 1½-quart casserole and bake in 350 degree oven for 30 minutes or until puffed and nicely browned. Serve immediately. Serves 4.

2	c milk
½	c Stone-Buhr cornmeal
1	tsp salt
¼	tsp baking powder
3	egg yolks
2	tbsp butter or margarine
3	egg whites

MUSHROOM PILAF

I like this pilaf because the wine gives it such a good flavor.

Clean mushrooms and slice. Cook mushrooms, green onion and garlic in margarine until vegetables are soft, but not browned. Add salt and cracked wheat. Stir in wine and water. Cover tightly and cook over low heat until tender, about 25 minutes. Remove cover and poke cubes of cheese into surface of hot pilaf. Serves 4.

½	lb fresh mushrooms
½	c chopped green onion
1	clove garlic, finely chopped
¼	c butter or margarine
1	tsp salt
1	c Stone-Buhr cracked wheat
1	c rose wine
½	c water
½	c cheddar cheese cubes (optional)

hint: In preparing salads, use salad dressings sparingly. Once tossed, each leaf should be lightly coated. Salad dressings are high in calories and too much dressing adds calories. Tear rather than cut salad greens. The greens look better and cutting them with a knife often causes the edges to turn brown.

BARLEY CASSEROLE

½ c margarine or butter
1 c chopped onions
1 c mushrooms, sliced
1½ c Stone-Buhr pearl barley
1 jar (2 oz) chopped pimentos, drained
¼ tsp salt
⅛ tsp pepper
3 c beef bouillon

This is a nice change from potatoes and rice. Barley is one of my favorite grains because it has a chewy texture.

Melt margarine in skillet. Add onions, mushrooms and barley. Cook on medium heat until lightly browned. Place in casserole. Stir in pimento, salt, pepper and bouillon. Cover and bake in 350 degree oven for 1 hour or until barley is tender. Yields 6 servings.

WHEAT PILAF

1 c Stone-Buhr cracked wheat
2 tbsp minced onion
2 tbsp butter or margarine
2 c chicken broth
¼ tsp oregano

The chicken broth and oregano make this a nice Pilaf recipe. Serve with pork or chicken.

Brown the wheat and onion lightly in butter over low heat, about 10 minutes. Pour in the broth and add oregano. Bring to a boil, lower heat, cover pot and simmer until liquid is absorbed, about 20 to 30 minutes. If it is not dry and fluffy, remove lid and heat for a few minutes until dry. Do not stir. Serves 4 to 6.

PARMESAN GNOCCHI

3 c milk
½ c butter or margarine
1 tsp salt
1 c +2½ tbsp Stone-Buhr whole wheat farina, uncooked
2 eggs, slightly beaten
2 c grated Parmesan cheese

If your oven is hot, bake these for only 10 minutes. Sometimes I serve the hot farina as it is without chilling it and forming into balls. It is good both ways.

Combine milk, butter and salt in saucepan. Scald, do not boil. Add farina in continuous stream stirring constantly. Cook, stirring until thickened. Beat in eggs and ½ of cheese. Chill until firm. Form into little balls with spoon and roll in remaining cheese. Bake in 425 degree oven until hot and brown, about 10-15 minutes. Serve with heated tomato sauce. Makes 8 servings.

VIENNA RICE

A delicious way to serve rice! I always make this when I'm serving veal. You can use white wine instead of ½ cup water, if you'd like.

Saute onion and rice in 1 tablespoon butter for 5 minutes; add seasoning, water and bouillon. Bring to a boil, stir once, cover and simmer 40 minutes or until tender. Add peas and butter and toss lightly. Sprinkle paprika on top and serve. Serves 6.

1	small onion, minced
1	c Stone-Buhr raw brown rice
1	tbsp butter
½	tsp salt
⅛	tsp pepper
2½	c beef bouillon
½	c water
1	c frozen peas
2	tbsp butter or margarine
1	tsp paprika

GREEN RICE

This is a delicious rice and spinach casserole. It is nice to serve at buffets because it is so attractive in color. Garnish it with pimento or hard cooked egg wedges.

Mix all ingredients well and place in 2 quart casserole. Bake at 325 degrees for 45 minutes. Yields 6 servings.

3	c cooked Stone-Buhr brown rice
¼	c grated Parmesan cheese
⅓	c chopped parsley
½	c minced cooked spinach
2	eggs, well beaten
1	c milk
¼	c melted butter or margarine
1½	tsp salt
1	tbsp Worcestershire sauce
2	tbsp minced onion

hint: To cook vegetables in water, use the smallest amount possible and cook them quickly. The best flavor in vegetables results when most of the cooking water is absorbed by the vegetables. Vegetables can be enhanced with herbs and spices. Onion, garlic and parsley can be added to any vegetable.

STEAMED MILLET with HERBS

1 c Stone-Buhr millet
3 c water
½ c chopped onions
2 tbsp oil
½ c chopped green pepper
1 tsp salt
½ tsp MSG (optional)
½ c warm water
½ tsp dill weed
1 tsp fresh basil (optional)

Millet has a very delicate flavor. This casserole is good with any main dish.

Cook millet (in covered saucepan) in 3 cups water until tender, about 35 minutes. Add more water if necessary. Saute onions in oil, add green pepper, salt and MSG. Add ½ cup water and cook 5 minutes. Combine onion and green pepper mixture with millet. Add sweet basil and dill weed. Cover and simmer for 2 to 5 minutes. Serves 4 to 6.

KASHA

1½ c Stone-Buhr wheat kernels
1 c Stone-Buhr millet
5 c water
1 c chopped onion
1½ c chopped celery
1 c diced green pepper
1 clove garlic, crushed
½ c chopped fresh mushrooms
2 tbsp shortening
1 tsp salt
1 tsp MSG

This is a favorite Russian dish. Sometimes buckwheat groats are used instead of wheat kernels. This is delicious hot as a side dish and cold as a salad. This recipe makes a lot—you might make just half of a recipe the first time.

Cook wheat kernels in 5 cups water in pressure cooker 15 minutes at 15 pounds pressure. Add millet to wheat kernels and cook 25 to 30 minutes in an uncovered pan. Drain any excess water. Brown onion, celery, green pepper, garlic and mushrooms in shortening. Add salt and MSG. Combine cooked millet and wheat kernels and vegetable mixture. Serve hot or cold. Serves 10.

HOT GERMAN SALAD

This is a delicious hot salad. Serve it with hot dogs or brat-wurst for a delicious light supper.

Fry bacon until crisp while rice cooks. Reserve ⅓ cup of bacon drippings in skillet. Combine reserved bacon fat, vinegar, sugar, salt, pepper, onion and celery seed, and heat, stirring until sugar is dissolved. Add green pepper and pimento. Pour over hot cooked rice. Add one egg, diced and crumbled bacon; mix lightly. Turn into serving dish and garnish with remaining egg, sliced. Serves about 6.

2½	c hot cooked Stone-Buhr brown rice
8	strips bacon
⅓	c bacon drippings
¼	c cider vinegar
¼	c sugar
½	tsp salt
⅛	tsp pepper
1	tbsp grated onion
¾	tsp celery seed
¼	c chopped green pepper
¼	c chopped pimento
2	hard cooked eggs

CARROT RAISIN SALAD

This is a nice variation of carrot salad.

Cook cracked wheat and rinse it with cold water. Drain well. Add French dressing and chill. Add remaining ingredients. Mix well and chill until ready to serve. Serve in lettuce cups. Serves 6.

2½	c Stone-Buhr cooked cracked wheat
2	tbsp French dressing
1½	c shredded carrots
¼	c raisins
⅓	c mayonnaise
½	tsp salt

SHRIMP and PINEAPPLE SALAD

Serve this salad in lettuce cups or in half a cantaloupe for a luncheon.

Cook rice. When tender, rinse with cold water and drain well. Drain and clean shrimp. Drain pineapple. Combine rice, shrimp, pineapple, celery, cabbage and pimento. Blend lemon juice, parsley and mayonnaise and combine lightly with rice mixture. Add salt and pepper. Chill thoroughly before serving. Serves 6.

2	c cooked Stone-Buhr brown rice
1	5 oz can small shrimp
1	8¾ oz can pineapple tidbits
½	c chopped celery
½	c chopped cabbage
¼	c chopped pimento
3	tbsp lemon juice
2	tbsp chopped parsley
½	c mayonnaise
	Salt and pepper to taste

TUNA SALAD

2/3 c Stone-Buhr brown rice
1 6½ or 7 oz can tuna, drained and broken into chunks
1 c shredded carrot
1 c diced celery
2 tbsp chopped onion
½ c mayonnaise or salad dressing
2 tsp lemon juice
¼ tsp Worcestershire sauce
¼ tsp salt
¼ tsp dried mixed salad herbs, crushed

Decorate this salad with carrot curls and serve on a bed of endive or shredded romaine. Rinsing the rice keeps the salad from being gummy.

Cook rice according to package directions; rinse with cold water and drain well. Add tuna, carrot, celery and onion; chill. At serving time add dressing made of mayonnaise, lemon juice, Worcestershire sauce, salt and herbs. Toss lightly and serve on a bed of lettuce. Makes 4 to 6 servings.

SHERWOOD SALAD

1 c cooked Stone-Buhr brown rice
1 1-lb can of kidney beans, drained and rinsed
2 hard cooked eggs, chopped
¼ c chopped onion
¼ c chopped celery
¼ c chopped green pepper
½ c sweet pickle relish
½ tsp salt
¼ tsp pepper
1/3 c mayonnaise
1 tsp vinegar

This salad is a good traveler and is ideal to take along to a potluck supper or picnic.

Rinse cooked rice with cold water. Drain well. Combine kidney beans with rice, eggs, onion, celery, green pepper and relish. Blend salt, pepper, mayonnaise and vinegar. Mix lightly with salad. Chill. Makes 6 servings.

POINSETTIA SALAD

This pretty salad is nice to serve during the holidays. Sometimes I press the salad into a ring mold and fill the center with relishes.

Cook rice according to package directions. Rinse with cold water and drain well. Combine tuna, rice, pecans, mayonnaise, lemon juice and tabasco sauce. Toss lightly until well mixed. Press into individual molds or use a ⅓ cup measure. Turn out onto a lettuce leaf. Cut petals from pimento and arrange on salads to resemble poinsettias. Makes 5 to 6 servings.

1	can (7 oz) chunk style tuna, drained
1	c cooked Stone-Buhr brown rice
½	c chopped pecans
⅓	c mayonnaise
1	tbsp lemon juice
¼	tsp tabasco sauce
1	canned whole pimento
	Salad greens

SUPPER SALAD

This salad is also good served in tomato cups. Scoop out the tomatoes, salt the inside lightly and allow them to drain about a half an hour before filling with the salad.

Cook rice according to package directions. Place in colander and rinse well with cold water; drain thoroughly. Place rice in bowl. Mix all ingredients, adding enough salad dressing to moisten. May be served on lettuce. Serves 4 to 6.

1	c Stone-Buhr brown rice
1	c diced luncheon meat
	Salt and pepper to taste
3	tbsp minced celery
1	tbsp minced onion
2	tbsp minced green pepper
	Salad dressing

TABBOULEH

This mid-eastern salad is very tangy. Serve only small amounts to each person. Let salad marinate at least ½ hour before serving. You may prefer to add more oil. Traditionally people also add chopped fresh mint (about 2 tablespoons).

Soak cracked wheat in cold water for about 10 minutes; drain. Wrap in cheese cloth and squeeze until dry. In large bowl combine cracked wheat, tomatoes, parsley, onion, lemon juice and salt by tossing lightly with a fork. Just before serving stir in oil.

½	c Stone-Buhr cracked wheat
3	med or 2 lg ripe fresh tomatoes, finely chopped
1	c finely chopped parsley
1	c finely chopped onion
⅓	c fresh lemon juice
2	tsp salt
1	tbsp oil

MAIN DISHES

Stuffed Game Hens with Orange Glaze p.65, Cornbread Dressing p.65

MAIN DISHES

This main dish section provides recipes that are high in protein. Each day we need an ample supply of protein to maintain good health.

We all know that meat and fish are good sources of protein but we often forget dried beans and dairy products, both of which are high protein foods. You will notice that each of the bean dishes in this book contains at least a small amount of milk, fish or meat. The addition of a small amount of animal protein makes the protein in beans such as soy beans more easily utilized by the body.

Whole grains such as soy beans and brown rice are rich in vitamins and minerals that your body needs. When you cook whole grain products, try to use just enough water to soften them so that little cooking liquid is left when they are done. Because soy beans are dried, they must be rehydrated before they become tender. Using a pressure cooker to cook beans helps to speed up cooking. When using a pressure cooker always be sure to include some fat in the beans so that the water does not foam and clog the vent.

Cheese has long been a source of protein in man's diet. Cheese in our diet dates back to the domestication of animals, about 9,000 B.C. It is referred to historically wherever animals produced more milk than people could use in fluid form.

Because there was no refrigeration cheese was made from all milk that was not used each day. The Greeks in ancient times trained Olympic athletes on diets of cheese and their traditional wedding cakes were made with cheese. Cheese was one of the foods that Caesar's legions carried with them as a mainstay. Cheeses can be used as a main dish for your family. Cheese souffles, au gratin potatoes with ham and cheese fondue are some of the favorite ways of letting cheese add protein to your diet.

Fish is a good source of protein. In general it is low in fat and delicious in flavor. Fish should be gutted as soon as possible after being caught. Fish are highly perishable and should always be kept in the coldest part of the refrigerator. If you want to keep fish frozen for longer than a day or two, it should be wrapped tightly in heavy freezer paper or heavy duty aluminum foil, then frozen. To save on freezer space, you can filet the fish. Leftover cooked fish can be flaked and mixed with mayonnaise and chopped green onions for a delicious sandwich spread.

SOY FLOUR MEAT LOAF

The soy flour and meat make this a nutritious main dish. This recipe is easy to cut in half for serving two.

Combine all ingredients and mix well. Shape and place in a 9 x 5-inch loaf pan. Bake at 350 degrees for 50 minutes or until done. Serve with tomato sauce, if desired. Makes 4 servings.

1	lb ground meat
2	eggs
1	c milk
2½	tsp salt
½	c Stone-Buhr soy flour
¼	c Stone-Buhr quick-cooking rolled oats
½	c minced onion
¼	tsp pepper

PORK MEAT BALLS
CANTONESE STYLE

Instead of frying the meatballs, this recipe bakes them. This is so easy and the meatballs keep their shape and get a nice crusty outside.

Combine pork, bread, onion, egg, milk, and seasonings. Shape into balls, using 1 tablespoon for each. Place in shallow baking pan and bake at 350 degrees for 40 minutes. Drain off excess fat. Drain pineapple, reserving liquid. Add enough water to make 1 cup. Mix together brown sugar, cornstarch, ginger and salt. Add pineapple liquid, vinegar and soy sauce.

Cook, stirring constantly until thickened. Add mixture to browned meat balls. Cook for about 5 minutes. Add celery, green pepper and pineapple. Cook just until heated through. Serve over hot Stone-Buhr long grain brown rice. Makes 6 servings.

Meat Balls:

1½	lbs ground pork
1	c Oroweat bread, crumbled
1	sm onion, chopped
1	egg, beaten
⅓	c milk
1½	tsp salt
¼	tsp dry mustard
⅛	tsp pepper

Sweet sour sauce:

1	can (13½ oz) pineapple tidbits
¼	c brown sugar
1½	tbsp cornstarch
½	tsp ginger
¼	tsp salt
¼	c vinegar
1	tbsp soy sauce

Vegetables:

1½	c diagonally-sliced celery
1	green pepper, cut julienne style

TAMALE-CHEESE PIE

Serve this with avocado salad and have a Mexican dinner. This tamale pie is delicious and very colorful.

Filling:
- ½ c chopped onion
- 1 clove garlic, minced
- 1 tbsp butter or margarine
- 1 lb ground beef
- 1 c sliced fresh mushrooms
- 1 1-lb can tomatoes
- 1 12-oz can whole kernel corn, drained
- 1 8-oz can tomato sauce
- ¼ c chopped green pepper
- 1 tbsp chili powder
- 1½ tsp salt
- 1 c sliced black olives

Crust:
- ¾ c Stone-Buhr cornmeal
- 3 c milk
- 1 tbsp butter or margarine
- 1 tsp salt
- 2 eggs, beaten
- 2 c shredded cheddar cheese

Saute onion and garlic in butter. Add beef and mushrooms; cook and stir until beef loses red color. Add tomatoes, corn, tomato sauce, green pepper, chili powder and salt. Cover and simmer 45 minutes. Add olives; simmer for 15 minutes longer. Set aside. For crust, combine and mix cornmeal and 1 cup milk. Combine remaining 2 cups milk, butter and salt; heat to boiling. Gradually add cornmeal mixture, stirring constantly; cook until thickened.

Cover and cook over very low heat for 15 minutes. Stir in eggs and 1 cup cheese. Continue stirring until cheese is melted. Line bottom of greased, shallow, 2 quart casserole with corn mixture, reserving 1½ cups for top. Pour meat filling over corn-meal mixture. Drop spoonfuls of remaining cornmeal mixture on top of meat. Sprinkle remaining 1 cup cheese over all. Bake at 350 degrees for 50 to 60 minutes or until brown and bubbly around edges. Serves 6.

MONDAY'S MEAT LOAF

This meat loaf is moist and flavorful. For a mustard sauce, combine equal parts of mustard and brown sugar.

- 1 lb hamburger
- ¼ c catsup
- ¼ c Stone-Buhr barley flakes
- 1 tsp salt
- 1 onion, chopped
- 2 eggs

Mix all ingredients together well. Shape in a 9x5-inch loaf pan and bake at 350 degrees for about 45 minutes or until done. Drain off drippings and serve topped with a mustard sauce, if desired. Makes 5 servings.

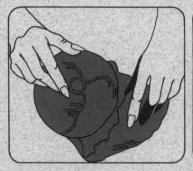 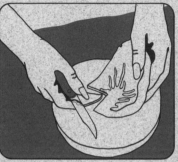 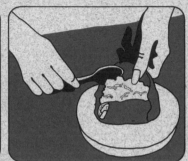 

When selecting a head of cabbage to make cabbage rolls, choose one that is not too solid as the leaves are easier to separate. Cutting out the thicker part of the leaves allows you to roll the cabbage and filling tightly, this helps keep the rolls together as they bake.

HUNGARIAN CABBAGE ROLLS

This is my favorite recipe for cabbage rolls. I like to serve these with caraway rye bread. These store well and taste even better when reheated.

Core cabbage. Place, core end down, in saucepan with 2 inches boiling water. Simmer until cabbage leaves are just soft enough to roll. Drain; cool. Carefully remove leaves. Combine beef, barley, onion, egg and seasonings; place in center of leaves, dividing evenly. Roll up, tucking in edges. In large baking pan, combine sauerkraut, half the tomato sauce, and brown sugar. Place cabbage rolls, seam side down, on sauerkraut. Pour remaining tomato sauce over rolls. Cover and bake at 350 degrees for 1 hour or until done. Serve with sour cream, if desired. Makes 6 servings.

1	large head cabbage
1	lb lean ground beef
1	c Stone-Buhr cooked barley
1	onion, chopped
1	egg, slightly beaten
1	tsp salt
½	tsp allspice
⅛	tsp garlic powder
1	can (27 oz) sauerkraut, drained
2	cans (8 oz each) tomato sauce
¼	c packed brown sugar
	Sour cream (optional)

STUFFED GREEN PEPPERS

½	c Stone-Buhr long grain brown rice
¼	tsp salt
8	med. green peppers
1	lb ground chuck
1	sm onion, minced
1	can (8 oz) tomato sauce
1	tsp salt

These green peppers are nice to serve for a buffet dinner because they are easy to serve. If your green peppers are large, slice them in half lengthwise rather than cutting off the tops.

Place rice in saucepan with 1½ cups water. Add ¼ teaspoon salt and bring to a boil. Cover and simmer until rice is tender, about 40 minutes. Cut tops off green peppers and scoop out seeds. Place upright in a baking dish. Mix together beef, onion, tomato sauce, salt, and cooked rice (all the water should be absorbed). Stuff green peppers and replace tops. Pour ½ cup water in bottom of baking dish and bake in a 350 degree oven for about 1 hour. Makes 8 servings.

EGGPLANT CASSEROLE

1	c Stone-Buhr brown rice
1	lg eggplant
1	onion, chopped
1	lb ground beef
1¾	c canned tomatoes, drained
½	c dry sherry or white wine
1	c grated Parmesan cheese
1½	tsp salt
¼	tsp pepper
1	tsp sugar
½	tsp MSG or Accent

A delicious variation for a hamburger casserole. Blanching the eggplant takes out the excess water and bitterness.

Add brown rice to 3 cups boiling salted water. Cover and cook about 35 minutes. Rice should be starting to get tender, but still slightly firm. Drain well. Pare and dice eggplant. Cover with boiling, salted water; let stand 5 minutes. Brown onion and ground beef. Add tomatoes and sherry; bring to a boil and simmer 5 minutes. Add drained eggplant, rice and all remaining ingredients. Transfer to a 3 quart buttered casserole or 2-1½ quart casseroles. Cover and bake at 350 degrees for 30 minutes. Remove cover; increase heat to 400 degrees. Bake 15 minutes or until golden brown on top. Serves 6-8.

PIZZA

How quick! This dough is rather thick but with all that filling you need it. Try making individual size pizzas next time.

Mix pancake mix and oil with a fork; add milk, mixing lightly. Place on a greased cookie sheet and form a 12-inch circle. Bake at 450 degrees for 10 minutes. Set aside.

Pan-fry pork sausage meat; drain. In some of the drippings brown onion till transparent. Add tomato sauce, tomato paste, salt, pepper, oregano and sausage. Cover and simmer 20 minutes.

Pour over baked crust; top with ½ cup shredded cheese. Return to oven till cheese melts. Sprinkle with grated Parmesan cheese before serving. Serves 4-6.

Dough:
- 1½ c Stone-Buhr pancake mix
- ¼ c oil
- ¼ c milk

Filling:
- 1 lb pork sausage meat
- ¾ c chopped onion
- 1 8 oz can tomato sauce
- 1 6 oz. can tomato paste
- ½ tsp salt
- ¼ tsp pepper
- ¼ tsp oregano
- 1 c shredded cheddar cheese
- ¼ c grated Parmesan cheese

BARBECUED BEEF BALLS

The sauce on these meatballs is very spicy. They are delicious when reheated.

Combine meat, oats, milk, onion, salt and pepper. Shape into balls. Roll in rice flour and brown in fat. Arrange in greased, 2 quart baking dish. Combine remaining ingredients. Pour over meat balls. Bake at 350 degrees for about 35 minutes. Serve over rice or wheat pilaf. Makes 6-8 servings.

- 1½ lbs. lean ground beef
- ¾ c Stone-Buhr rolled oats
- 1 c milk
- 1 tbsp minced onion
- 1½ tsp salt
- ⅛ tsp pepper
- Stone-Buhr brown or white rice flour
- 3 tbsp fat
- 2 tbsp sugar
- 2 tbsp Worcestershire Sauce
- 1 c catsup
- ½ c water
- ¼ c vinegar
- ½ c minced onion

HAM-RICE PINWHEELS

2   3-oz pkg cream cheese
1   c cooked Stone-Buhr brown rice
6   tbsp finely chopped olives
3   tbsp grated onion
1½   tbsp horseradish
1   tbsp pickle relish
1   tsp Worcestershire sauce
6-8   thin slices boiled ham

These are delicious! Try varying the filling by adding chopped nuts or one of your favorite herbs or spices.

Let cream cheese soften at room temperature; beat until fluffy. Stir in remaining ingredients except the ham; blend well. Spread ham slices with mixture and roll tightly. Skewer with toothpicks; cover and chill several hours. At serving time, cut into 1-inch pieces. Serve as an appetizer or on lettuce as a salad. Makes 3 dozen.

APPETIZER MEAT BALLS

¾   lb ground beef
¼   lb ground pork
¾   c Stone-Buhr cereal mates
¼   c finely chopped water chestnuts
¼   tsp Worcestershire sauce
½   c milk
½   tsp garlic salt
     Few drops of tabasco
     Margarine or butter

This is another meatball variation to use with cocktails. Try baking the meatballs instead of browning them in a fry pan.

Combine all ingredients except margarine; mix well. Shape into small balls. Brown well in margarine; drain on paper towels. Place in a chafing dish. Cover with sweet sour or barbecue sauce, if desired. Use toothpicks to serve. Makes about 75 meatballs.

SESAME CHEESE BALLS

1   3-oz pkg cream cheese, softened
¼   c blue cheese
¼   c minced dried beef
     Dash cayenne pepper
¼   c toasted Stone-Buhr sesame seeds

These are nice to serve as appetizers. I sometimes garnish molded salads with them as well.

Blend cheeses with dried beef and seasoning. Shape in small balls. Chill. Roll in sesame seeds. Makes 20 small balls.

PARTY CHEESE BALLS

Plan on serving this as an appetizer at your next party. This cheese spread is my favorite to serve with melba toast and fresh ripe pears for dessert.

Toast seeds in 350 degree oven about 15 minutes. Soak beef base in lemon juice. Mix together all ingredients except sesame seeds. Shape mixture into 1 or 2 balls. Spread seeds on waxed paper and roll cheese balls to coat. Chill thoroughly. Serve surrounded by assorted crackers.

½   c Stone-Buhr sesame seeds
2   tsp beef flavor base or dry bouillon
¼   c lemon juice
1   lb medium sharp cheddar cheese, shredded
¼   c minced onion or 1 tbsp onion flakes
¼   c mayonnaise
2   tbsp catsup
2   tbsp Worcestershire sauce
2   tsp dry mustard

BAKED FISH GOURMET

You can use any white fish in this recipe. Sometimes I substitute ¼ cup dry white wine for part of the milk.

Stir cracked wheat and salt into boiling water and cover pan. Cook over low heat about 20 minutes. Remove from heat and let stand covered for 5 to 10 minutes. Spread in 9 x 13-inch baking dish. Top with fish fillets.

Heat butter and onion until frothy in frying pan. Blend in flour, ½ teaspoon salt, pepper and dry mustard. Remove from heat and stir in milk and Worcestershire. Return to heat and stir constantly until mixture thickens and comes to a boil. Pour sauce over fish and cracked wheat. Sprinkle with grated cheese. Bake uncovered at 350 degrees for 30 to 35 minutes. Serves 8.

½   c Stone-Buhr cracked wheat
¼   tsp salt
1¾   c boiling water
1½   lbs fish fillets
Sauce:
2   tbsp butter or margarine
1   tbsp chopped onion
2   tbsp flour
½   tsp salt
⅛   tsp pepper
½   tsp dry mustard
1   c milk
½   tsp Worcestershire Sauce
1   c grated cheddar cheese

FRENCH BEANS

2 c Stone-Buhr soy beans
¼-½ lb salt pork, diced
3 tbsp butter or margarine
½ lb fresh pork sausage
2 garlic sausages, sliced
(smoked type, such as
Polish, etc.)
2 onions
1 clove garlic, minced
1 lb ground chuck
1 tsp salt
Freshly ground pepper
1 c dry white wine
1 c tomato sauce
1 c bean cooking liquid
½ tsp dried thyme
1 c coarse dry bread crumbs
2 tbsp chopped parsley

This can be used as a main dish or side dish. It is similar to a French cassoulet.

Soak beans in 2 quarts of water 4 or 5 hours. Add an onion stuck with 2 cloves, bay leaf, a sprig of parsley and salt pork. Simmer gently until tender, about 1½ hours. Season last half hour with 1 to 1½ teaspoons salt. Drain beans and reserve 1 cup cooking liquid. In a frypan, heat 1 tablespoon butter. Add sausages. When fat begins to cook out, add onion and garlic. Stir and fry till lightly browned. Drain excess fat. Add ground beef. Cook only till it loses red color. Season with salt and pepper. In a 3-quart casserole, put half the drained beans, top with half the meat mixture, repeat layers. To frying pan add white wine, tomato sauce, 1 cup bean liquid and thyme. Heat to simmering, pour over layers of meat and beans. Stir gently with fork so liquid runs throughout. Bake in 350 degree oven 1 hour. Heat remaining 2 tablespoons butter till frothy. Stir in crumbs and parsley. Mix and spread over casserole. Bake 30 minutes. Makes 8 servings.

SAVORY BEAN STEW

1 c dry Stone-Buhr soy beans
1 qt water
⅓ c chopped onion
1 tbsp fat
½ lb ground beef
2 to 2½ c cooked tomatoes
(No. 303 can)
Salt and pepper to taste

You can add a little more water to this and serve it as a soup if you prefer.

Wash beans; put into water and boil for 2 minutes. Cover and let stand for 1 hour. Simmer 1 to 1½ hours or until almost tender, adding more water as necessary. Brown onion in fat. Add meat, stir and cook slowly for a few minutes. Combine all ingredients. Simmer until meat is tender and the flavors are blended, about 30 minutes. Season to taste. Serves 5.

SOY BEANS with FISH

The flavorful soy beans are a nice accompaniment to the fried fish. I sometimes serve this in individual casserole dishes.

Fry bacon. Put dry soy beans on top. Pour in wine and add water to cover. Add salt, pepper and bay leaves. Allow to soak overnight. The next day, cook in pressure cooker about 30 minutes at 15 pounds pressure. (If necessary, add a small amount of water before cooking). Beans will now be tender. Roll fish in egg and then in bread crumbs. Fry in margarine until nicely browned and tender.

Boil off any excess liquid from beans. Remove bay leaves, place in heated serving dish and arrange fish on top. Garnish with chopped green onion, minced red pepper and chopped parsley. Makes 8 servings.

¼	lb sliced bacon
2	c dry Stone-Buhr soy beans
2	c dry white wine
	Salt and pepper to taste
2	sm bay leaves
1½	lbs fish fillets
1	egg, beaten
	Bread crumbs
¼	c butter or margarine
2	green onions, chopped
1	hot red pepper, minced
2	tbsp chopped parsley

ALMOND CHICKEN

This is a delicious way to serve chicken. You'll like the way the almonds stay on the chicken in this recipe.

Mix first 4 ingredients. Add chicken and coat. Then dip in combined egg and milk. Coat with almonds and place, skin side down, on lightly oiled, foil-lined pan. Drizzle with butter and sprinkle generously with salt. Bake in 375 degrees oven 30 minutes, turn skin side up and bake 40 minutes longer, or until well browned. Makes 4 servings.

½	c Stone-Buhr potato starch
1	tsp salt
⅛	tsp pepper
1	tsp paprika
1	frying chicken, about 2½ lbs. cut up
1	egg, slightly beaten
2	tbsp milk
1	c finely chopped almonds
2	tbsp butter or margarine, melted
	Salt

STUFFED GAME HENS
with ORANGE GLAZE

4 game hens
1 pkg Oroweat Corn Bread dressing mix
¼ lb butter or margarine
1 medium onion, chopped
1 c water or chicken bouillon
¼ tsp basil
1½ tsp Worcestershire sauce
1 tsp salt
¼ tsp pepper
1 egg, beaten
1 (6-oz) can frozen orange juice concentrate, thawed
2 tbsp soy sauce

These game hens make a festive main dish. The orange glaze is deep, rich and flavorful. If the birds get too brown before they are done, make a loose foil tent to cover them during the remaining roasting time.

Defrost game hens and rinse thoroughly. In a bowl, place one package corn bread dressing mix. Set aside. Melt the butter in a saucepan, add onion and saute for 2 or 3 minutes. Add water or chicken bouillon, basil, Worcestershire sauce, salt and pepper. Mix well and pour over corn bread dressing mix. Add egg and 3 tbsp of orange juice concentrate and mix the dressing well.

Stuff game hens loosely with dressing and place them on a rack in roasting pan. Bake in a 350 degree oven for 20 minutes. To the remaining orange juice concentrate, stir in the soy sauce; baste the game hens. Continue baking for 45 minutes, basting frequently. Serve additional sauce or reserve it to use on another day. Makes 4 generous servings.

CRISPY FRIED CHICKEN

1 c Stone-Buhr cornmeal
2 tsp salt
½ tsp garlic salt
¼ tsp pepper
1 egg, slightly beaten
1 tbsp water
2 3-lb frying chickens, quartered
Shortening

Chicken breaded with cornmeal is very crispy. I usually serve it with scalloped potatoes.

Combine cornmeal, salt, garlic salt and pepper in a sack. Shake thoroughly. Combine egg and water. Dip chicken pieces in egg mixture. Shake each piece of chicken in sack until coated. Pan fry in large fry pan in hot shortening about ½-inch deep, until golden brown on all sides. Reduce heat; cover and cook about 40 minutes or until tender. For crisper chicken, uncover last 10 minutes. 8 servings.

CHICKEN ENCHILADAS

Enchiladas are delicious—if you do not have time to make your own tortillas, buy frozen ones that are available in the supermarkets.

For filling, mix chicken, cheese, olives and ¼ cup chopped onion. In saucepan, mix tomato sauce, remaining onion, chili powder and garlic; simmer for 5 minutes. Place about ¼ cup filling in center of each tortilla, then roll up. Place, seam side down, in one layer in shallow baking dish. Cover with sauce. Sprinkle with additional grated cheese. Bake at 350 degrees for 15 to 20 minutes.

Pour hot water over cornmeal. Cover and set aside. Beat the eggs in a bowl for 1 minute. Add the skim milk, whole wheat flour and all-purpose flour to the eggs. Add cornmeal and water and blend until smooth. Heat a lightly oiled 6-inch skillet. Pour in enough batter to thinly cover the bottom of the skillet, tip both ways for even thickness. Bake on both sides until golden brown. Yield: makes 12 small tortillas.

2	c diced cooked chicken or turkey
1	c grated cheddar cheese
½	c chopped ripe olives (optional)
½	c chopped onion
2	cans (8 oz each) tomato sauce
2	tsp chili powder
1	clove garlic, minced
12	tortillas (see below)
	More grated cheddar cheese

Tortillas:
1	c hot water
½	c Stone-Buhr cornmeal
2	eggs
1½	c skim milk
1	c Stone-Buhr whole wheat flour
1	c Stone-Buhr all-purpose flour

SESAME CHICKEN ⓐ

If you like sesame seeds as well as I do, this is a fantastic recipe. The potato starch does a nice job of holding all of the seeds on. This chicken is also good cold.

Brush chicken with the butter. Coat with combined starch and salt and dip in egg beaten with 2 tablespoons water. Roll in sesame seed and put on lightly oiled, foil-lined baking pan. Bake in 400 degrees oven for 1 hour, or until browned. Makes 4 servings.

1	frying chicken, cut up
3	tbsp butter or margarine, melted
⅓	c Stone-Buhr potato starch
½	tsp salt
1	egg
⅔	c Stone-Buhr sesame seed

CHICKEN PARMIGIANO

3 lb chicken, cut up
1 egg, beaten
¼ c bread crumbs
¼ c Stone-Buhr potato starch
¼ c Stone-Buhr bran flakes
¼ c Parmesan cheese, grated
¼ c parsley, chopped
2 tsp salt
⅛ tsp pepper
¼ tsp garlic salt
¼ tsp savory
⅔ c butter or margarine, melted

This is an excellent breaded chicken recipe. Potato starch gives all meat breadings a full-bodied flavor. Try using this breading on fish also.

Combine dry ingredients, cheese, and seasonings. Dip chicken pieces in egg then in crumb mixture. Arrange the breaded chicken in a shallow baking pan in a single layer. Drizzle melted butter over chicken pieces. Bake, uncovered in a 350 degree oven for 1 hour, or until tender. Makes 4 servings.

ROAST CHICKEN
with BARLEY STUFFING

¾ c Stone-Buhr pearl barley
3 tsp salt
¾ tsp freshly ground black pepper
1 tsp paprika
2 cloves garlic, minced
2 3-lb chickens or 1,5-lb roasting hen
3 tbsp shortening
2 onions, chopped
1 carrot, sliced
2 stalks celery, sliced
3 sprigs parsley, chopped
6 slices Oroweat white bread, cubed and toasted

I think you'll like the dressing for this chicken recipe because it is moist and flavorful. The barley gives it some chewiness, which I think is nice in a dressing. This is also good in turkey or game hens.

Soak barley and cook according to package directions. Mix 1½ teaspoons of the salt, ½ teaspoon of the pepper, the paprika, and garlic together. Rub into the outside of chicken. Melt the shortening in a skillet. Add the onions, carrot, celery and parsley. Saute for 10 minutes stirring frequently. Add the cubed bread, barley and remaining salt and pepper. Mix together. Stuff chicken loosely with mixture (do not pack); close opening with thread, skewers or aluminum foil. Place on rack in roasting pan. Roast in 350 degree oven for 1½-2 hours or until browned and tender. Serves 6 to 8.

COCONUT-CURRY CHICKEN

For all curry lovers. This is a tangy chicken dish that is the most beautiful golden color when baked. Try serving it with bright green vegetables and boiled potatoes or rice.

Mix together orange juice concentrate, salt and egg. Add chicken and marinate 15 minutes. Remove chicken; reserve marinade. Mix bran flakes, cereal mates, coconut and curry powder and coat chicken with mixture, pressing it on. Place on lightly oiled, foil-lined pan and drizzle with butter combined with reserved marinade. Cover pan with foil and bake in moderate oven (350 degrees) 30 minutes. Uncover and bake 30 to 40 minutes longer, or until well browned. Serve on platter with garnish of orange slices. Makes 6 servings.

1/3	c frozen orange-juice concentrate, thawed
1	tsp salt
1	egg, slightly beaten
6	pieces of chicken, breasts or thighs
1/2	c Stone-Buhr bran flakes
1/2	c Stone-Buhr cereal mates
1/2	c shredded coconut
1	tsp curry powder
1/4	c butter or margarine, melted
	Orange slices

WHEAT GERM CHICKEN
with PEACHES

This dish is especially nice for buffet parties as it can be prepared ahead of time, and can wait in a warm oven until your guests are ready to eat.

Mix brown rice flour, salt, and pepper and coat chicken with the mixture. Dip in egg beaten with 2 tablespoons melted butter. Coat with 3/4 cup wheat germ. Put on lightly oiled, foil-lined pan and bake at 400 degrees for 25 minutes. Meanwhile, brush peach halves with remaining butter and coat with remaining wheat germ. Arrange in pan with chicken and bake 20 minutes longer. Makes 4 servings.

1/4	c Stone-Buhr brown rice flour
1	tsp salt
1/8	tsp pepper
1	frying chicken, about 2½ lbs, cut up
1	egg, slightly beaten
3	tbsp butter or margarine, melted
1	c Stone-Buhr wheat germ
1	can (1 lb) peach halves, drained

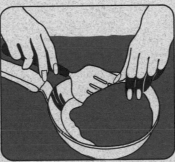

Crepes or thin pancakes are easy to make when you start with pancake mix. They make a festive and special container for creamed meats and fish.

FILLED CREPES with CHEESE

If you have any filling left, spoon it over the crepes before adding the cheese and paprika. This is delicious.

Beat together ingredients for the crepes. Add 2 tablespoons batter to lightly-buttered 7-inch skillet (tilt pan to cover bottom evenly). Brown lightly on both sides, turning once. Repeat until all batter is used. Saute mushrooms in butter; blend in flour and seasonings. Add milk. Cook, stirring constantly, until thickened. Stir in meat and parsley. Spoon about 1 tablespoon filling in center of each pancake. Roll; place in a shallow baking dish. Dot with butter; sprinkle with cheese and paprika. Bake at 400 degrees for 10 minutes. Makes 8 servings.

Crepes:
- 1   c milk
- 6   large eggs
- 1   c Stone-Buhr buckwheat pancake mix

Filling:
- ¼   lb mushrooms, chopped fine
- 2   tbsp each: butter or margarine, flour
- ½   tsp salt
- ¼   tsp pepper
- 1½ c milk, scalded
- 2   c diced cooked meat or tuna
- 1   tbsp minced parsley
- 1   tbsp butter or margarine
- 1   c grated swiss cheese
    Paprika

SEATTLE OYSTER PIE

Oysters and curry are such a nice combination. Sometimes I use a whole wheat flour pastry for a nice change. Be sure the pastry is rolled thin enough or it will not brown readily.

Cook potatoes in the boiling salted water until just tender; drain and set aside. In a frying pan, saute onion and celery in butter until onion is transparent. Stir in curry powder and flour and cook until bubbly. Gradually add milk, and cook, stirring until thickened. Season with salt, pepper, parsley and basil. Stir in the cooked potatoes. Cut oysters into bite-sized pieces and blend into the potato mixture. Turn mixture into a 9-inch square baking dish; top with eggs. Roll out pastry into about a 10-inch square; fit over eggs in baking dish and press to edge of dish to seal. Slash with a knife in several places to allow steam to escape. Bake in a 425 degree oven for 30 minutes, until crust is golden. Serve at once. Makes 4-5 servings.

3	c diced, peeled potatoes
	Boiling, salted water
1	small onion, chopped
1	stalk celery, thinly sliced
3	tbsp butter or margarine
½	tsp curry powder
2	tbsp Stone-Buhr potato starch
1	c milk
½	tsp salt
⅛	tsp pepper
1	tbsp chopped parsley
1	tsp whole basil, crushed
1	jar (10 oz) small Pacific oysters, well drained
4	hard-cooked eggs, quartered
	Pastry for a 1 crust pie

CRAB CASSEROLE DELUXE

This is a delicious seafood casserole. It is very rich and filling. Sometimes I place the crab meat mixture in scalloped shells to bake and serve.

Mix all ingredients except wheat germ, bread, and melted butter. Toss wheat germ, crumbled bread and butter together and divide in half. Combine one-half with crab mixture and pour into a greased 2-quart casserole. Top with remaining crumb mixture. Bake uncovered at 350 degrees for 40 minutes or until bubbling. Garnish with parsley, if desired. Serves 6.

1	lb crab meat
2	hard-cooked eggs, chopped
¾	c mayonnaise
1	onion, minced
½	c chopped parsley
3	tbsp lemon juice
2	tbsp Worcestershire sauce
1	tbsp prepared mustard
¼	c dry sherry
½	c Stone-Buhr wheat germ
1	c fresh Oroweat bread, crumbled
3	tbsp melted butter or margarine

SAUCED TUNA CASSEROLE

2   cans tuna (7½ oz each)
1   stalk celery, chopped
2   eggs
1   c Stone-Buhr oats or Stone-Buhr rice flakes
¾   c milk
1   tbsp lemon juice
½   tsp salt
    Dash of pepper
Onion Sauce
⅓   c chopped onion
2   tbsp butter or margarine
2   tbsp flour
1   c milk
    Salt and pepper to taste

This is a good recipe to prepare when you have unexpected guests for dinner. Rice flakes make this casserole a little firmer, rolled oats a little softer.

Drain tuna and place in a bowl. Add remaining ingredients. Mix well. Place in a greased 1½ quart casserole and bake at 350 degrees for about 50 minutes. Top with onion sauce. To make the sauce, chop onion finely and cook in margarine until onion is tender. Slowly stir in flour. Stir in milk. Cook over medium heat, stirring constantly until sauce comes to a boil. Boil one minute. Add salt and pepper. Pour some sauce over each serving of casserole. Makes 5 servings.

CHEESE STRATA

12   slices of Oroweat Old Style Country Bread
2   tbsp butter or margarine
½   lb cheddar cheese, thinly sliced
    Paprika
6   eggs
3   c milk
½   tsp salt
¼   tsp cayenne
6   tomato slices

This is almost like a cheese souffle, but only half the work. You can prepare it ahead of time and bake it just before serving. Try it for your next brunch!

Butter a 9 x 13-inch baking dish. Spread remaining butter on bread. Line bottom of baking dish with six slices of bread. Top with layer of cheese. Repeat layer, ending with cheese. Sprinkle liberally with paprika. Beat eggs well and add milk, salt and cayenne. Pour evenly over bread and cheese, being sure to moisten each slice of bread thoroughly. Refrigerate 1½ hours or overnight. Bake at 325 degrees 35 minutes; top with tomato slices and bake 10 to 15 minutes longer. To serve, cut into squares. Makes 6 servings.

HOT CRAB SOUFFLE

This is a nice dish to prepare for guests because you can get it all ready to put in the oven earlier in the day. I sometimes make this casserole in individual ramekins.

Dice 4 slices of the bread. Put in baking dish with crab, mayonnaise, onion, green pepper and celery. Trim crusts of remaining bread and place on top. Combine eggs and milk and pour over. Refrigerate overnight. Bake in a 325 degree oven for 15 minutes. Pour soup over top of casserole and top with cheese. Return to the oven and bake for 1 hour at 325 degrees. Garnish with paprika. Makes 6 servings.

8	slices Oroweat bread
2	c crab meat
½	c mayonnaise
1	c chopped onion
1	c chopped green pepper
1	c chopped celery
3	c milk
4	eggs, beaten
1	can mushroom soup, undiluted
¼	c grated cheddar cheese
	Paprika

SALMON STUFFED PEPPERS

You can prepare this with left-over cooked salmon (about 2 cups). If you prefer, you can use a white sauce instead of tomato sauce.

Cook barley according to package directions. Cut peppers lengthwise in half; scoop out seeds and membrane. Cook in boiling, salted water for about 2 minutes; drain. Meanwhile, combine salmon, barley, egg, cheese, onion, Worcestershire sauce, and salt. Place pepper halves in shallow baking dish; fill with salmon mixture. Pour tomato sauce over tops. Bake at 350 degrees for 30 minutes. Makes 6 servings.

1	c cooked Stone-Buhr barley
3	large green peppers
1	can (1 lb) salmon, drained, flaked
1	egg, slightly beaten
1	c processed American cheese cubes (¼-inch cubes)
1	tsp instant minced onion
½	tsp Worcestershire sauce
¼	tsp salt
1	can (8 oz) tomato sauce

LAMB SHANKS and BARLEY EN CASSEROLE

1 clove garlic
2 onions
2 carrots
Tops of 2 stalks of celery
4 sprigs parsley
3 tbsp olive oil
6 lamb shanks
Salt and pepper
2 c Stone-Buhr pearl barley
1¼ c consomme
1 c dry white wine
1 bay leaf
1 pinch thyme

Although this recipe is a slow cooking one, it's one of my favorites. The barley flavor combines well with the consomme and white wine. Serve with a crisp green salad.

Chop the garlic, onions, carrots, celery tops and parsley very fine. Saute in 2 tablespoons olive oil in a heavy 3 quart casserole until onions are transparent and golden. Remove vegetables from pan and set aside. Season lamb with salt and pepper. Brown in casserole. Meanwhile, heat remaining olive oil in another pan and add the barley. Stir constantly until golden tan.

Pour on consomme and wine, add bay leaf and thyme, then add to lamb shanks with vegetables. Add more liquid if necessary to cover barley. Bake in 300 degree oven for 2½ to 3 hours. When done, the barley should be barely moist and the meat tender. Serves 3 to 6.

BREADED PORK CHOPS

8 large pork chops
1 egg
2 tbsp water
½ c Stone-Buhr potato starch
2 tbsp Stone-Buhr cornmeal
2 tbsp Stone-Buhr cereal mates
2 tsp garllc salt
1 tsp salt
½ tsp pepper
¼ c oil

This breading has a nutlike flavor from the cereal mates and cornmeal. Be sure not to crowd the pan when you are browning the chops so they will brown evenly.

Trim extra fat off pork chops. Beat egg slightly with 2 tablespoons of water and set aside. Combine dry ingredients and mix well. Dip chops into egg and then into crumb mixture. Heat oil in a large, heavy skillet. Brown chops on both sides and continue cooking until done, about 25 minutes. Makes 4-8 servings.

SHERRIED VEAL with MUSHROOMS

This delicious recipe is one of my favorites. Be sure to blend flour with the sour cream as noted. This helps keep the sour cream from curdling.

Mix together potato starch, MSG, garlic powder, onion powder, salt and pepper. Roll veal cubes in seasoned flour. Heat the oil in a heavy skillet, add veal and brown slowly. Then add the sherry and water.

Cover and simmer until meat is tender, about 35 minutes. Add fresh mushrooms and rosemary and simmer 10 minutes more. Just before serving, mix the sour cream, flour and parsley together. Add to veal and bring to a boil. Serve over hot Stone-Buhr long grain brown rice or hot cracked wheat. Makes 4-6 servings.

1½	lbs veal, cut in cubes
¼	c Stone-Buhr potato starch
1	tsp MSG or Accent
⅛	tsp garlic powder
½	tsp onion powder
½	tsp salt
⅛	tsp pepper
3	tbsp oil
½	c sherry (dry)
½	c water
½	lb fresh mushrooms
⅛	tsp rosemary
½	c sour cream
1	tbsp Stone-Buhr all-purpose flour
1	tbsp parsley

GLAZED PORK with ORANGE WHEAT

An African way to serve pork. Excellent for those who love the flavor of limes and oranges. I like the flavor of thyme; start out by using only ¼ teaspoon if the flavor is new to you.

In a heavy skillet, heat the oil. Add pork cubes and brown. Stir in the onions, orange juice, lemon or lime juice, water, thyme, salt and pepper. Bring to a boil over high heat, cover, lower heat and simmer for 30 minutes. Then uncover the pan, raise heat to high and, stirring frequently to prevent burning, cook until the sauce forms a syrupy glaze.

Combine all ingredients for orange wheat and bring to a boil. Cook for 10 minutes. Then pour in a strainer and run hot water over the cooked cereal until the grains are separated. Place in center of platter and top with glazed pork. Serves 4 to 5.

¼	c oil
2	lbs lean pork, cut in 1-inch cubes
1½	c chopped onions
1	c orange juice
¼	c lime or lemon juice
¼	c water
½	tsp thyme (optional)
½	tsp salt
¼	tsp pepper

Orange Wheat:

1	c Stone-Buhr cracked wheat
1	c orange juice
2	c water
¼	tsp salt

PINEAPPLE SWISS STEAK

1   round steak (3 lbs), cut 1½-inches
    thick
⅓   c Stone-Buhr potato starch
1½ tsp salt
1   tsp paprika
¼   c shortening
1   can (20 oz) pineapple rings
    Water
1   envelope (1⅜ oz) onion soup mix
1   green pepper, cut into thick rings
1   tomato, cut into eighths
1   tbsp Stone-Buhr potato starch
¼   c cold water

This is a good recipe to serve to your family or company. The onion soup mix and pineapple give this a rich, fruity flavor. Serve with hot Stone-Buhr brown rice or hot cracked wheat.

Place meat on a cutting board. Cover with seasoned potato starch; pound with meat hammer or edge of a heavy plate. Turn steak several times, pounding until all the flour is taken up by the meat. Brown on both sides in shortening. Drain pineapple, reserving juice. Add enough water to juice to make 2 cups liquid. Blend liquid with onion soup mix; pour over steak. Cover and simmer for about 1 hour, or until meat is tender. Top with pineapple rings, green pepper and tomato during last 10 minutes of cooking time. Place meat on a heated platter. Blend potato starch with cold water and add to cooking liquid. Cook until slightly thickened, stirring constantly. Pour over meat. Serves 8.

hint: Ground beef is a very perishable food. After purchasing at the store it will stay fresh in the refrigerator only a maximum of two days. For longer storage, ground beef should be frozen. I usually store a few small packages of cooked ground beef. These are nice to have on hand. They can be added frozen to a pizza or spaghetti sauce. Cook ground beef and spread it out on a cookie sheet covered with waxed paper. Place in freezer for about one hour. Remove from freezer and break apart small pieces of the cooked ground beef. Place in a plastic bag and return to freezer. This can be used for quick pizzas made with tomato sauce and Oroweat English Muffins.

MINESTRONE VEGETABLE SOUP

An old family recipe. This recipe makes almost a gallon of soup. If you don't have a large family, perhaps you might want to share some of it with your neighbors.

Soak beans overnight in chicken stock. Saute onions and salt pork in butter, add beans and chicken stock (dry seasonings may be added at this time). Simmer for 1½ hours adding additional water if necessary. Add leeks, carrots, potatoes, celery and rice. Cook for 20 minutes. Add peas, zucchini and tomatoes. Cook until tender. Remove bay leaf; garnish with basil, parsley, garlic, Parmesan cheese and wine, if desired. Serves 8-12.

½	c Stone-Buhr soy beans
2	qts chicken stock or bouillon
¼	c butter
2	tbsp finely chopped onions
2	oz salt pork, diced
½	c finely chopped leeks
1	c diced carrots
1	c diced potatoes
⅓	c thinly sliced celery
½	c Stone-Buhr brown rice
1	bay leaf or 1 tsp rosemary
2	sprigs parsley or 2 tsp dried parsley
1	tsp salt
¼	tsp freshly ground pepper
1	c fresh green peas (1 lb unshelled)
1	c diced or sliced, unpeeled but scrubbed, zucchini
2	c drained, canned whole-pack tomatoes, coarsely chopped

Garnish:

1	tbsp finely cut fresh basil or 1 tsp dried basil, crumbled
1	tbsp finely chopped fresh parsley or 1 tsp dried
½	tsp finely chopped garlic
½	c freshly grated imported Parmesan cheese
1	tbsp wine per serving may also be added

SCOTCH BROTH

1 tbsp vegetable oil
2 lbs lamb neck slices
8 c boiling water
1 bay leaf
1 tbsp salt
1/8 tsp pepper
1/2 c Stone-Buhr pearl barley
1/2 c sliced onion
1 c chopped celery stalks and leaves
1 c sliced carrots
1 16 oz can tomatoes
1 clove garlic, minced
1/4 c chopped parsley

I like Scotch broth and, with lamb available most of the year, you can prepare it almost any time. Be sure that all the fat is skimmed off, as that is what often gives dishes with lamb a strong flavor.

Heat oil in a Dutch oven over moderately high heat; brown lamb lightly. Drain off excess fat. Add water, bay leaf, salt and pepper. Cover and simmer over low heat 1½ hours, adding additional water if necessary. Cool and chill several hours or overnight. Skim fat from top of soup and discard.

Add barley. Cover, bring to a boil over moderately high heat; reduce heat to moderately low and cook ½ hour. Add onion, celery, carrots, tomatoes and garlic; cook 45 minutes longer. Remove meat from bones, cut into large pieces and return to soup. Remove bay leaf and stir in parsley just before serving. If soup to too thick, thin with a little water, chicken bouillon or wine. Makes 2 quarts. Serves 6 to 8.

HAMBURGER-VEGETABLE CHOWDER

1/2 lb ground beef
2 tbsp butter or margarine
1 c canned tomatoes
1/2 c diced carrots
1/2 c diced celery
1 medium onion, chopped
1/2 tsp salt
1/4 tsp pepper
1/4 c Stone-Buhr pearl barley
1 c cubed potatoes
1½ qts. water

A really simple soup that is easy to make. You can add any leftover vegetables you have to it.

Brown meat in margarine. Add remaining ingredients and simmer until barley is tender (about 1 hour) or cook in pressure cooker at 15 lbs. pressure for about 15 minutes. Makes 4 servings.

HUNGARIAN BEAN SOUP
with NOODLE SQUARES

This is a delicious home-made soup. If you'd like, you can omit the noodles, although I think you'll enjoy making them. Be sure you roll them thin enough.

Cover beans with cold water; let stand overnight. Drain. Add 1½ quarts water, beef broth, tomato paste, vegetables and seasonings. Cover and simmer for 2 hours adding more water if soup gets too thick.

To make noodles: make "well" in flour; add egg and 2 tablespoons water. Mix until smooth. Knead on floured surface until dough does not stick to fingers. Roll out ⅛-inch thick. Cut into small squares or diamonds. When beans are tender, drop noodles into simmering soup; cook until noodles float. Score meat or cut into chunks; add to soup. Heat through. Serve with cucumber salad, cream dressing, dark bread and apple strudel. Makes 6 servings.

1	lb Stone-Buhr soy beans
	Water
1	c beef broth
1	can (6 oz) tomato paste
2	carrots, sliced
1	c celery, chopped
1	onion, chopped
2	tsp salt
½	tsp paprika
⅛	tsp pepper
1	c + 2 tbsp Stone-Buhr all-purpose flour
1	egg, beaten
1	knockwurst ring or 4 individual knockwurst (about 1 lb)

DRIED MUSHROOM SOUP

This is just like the soup my grandmother used to make. Dried mushrooms are available in most large supermarkets. They are very expensive, but you only need a very small amount.

Wash mushrooms thoroughly (you must use dried mushrooms). Combine mushrooms, barley, water, salt and pepper in a saucepan. Bring to a boil. Cover and cook over low heat for 1½ hours. Melt shortening in a skillet. Add the onions and saute for 10 minutes, stirring frequently. Add the flour, stirring until brown. Add flour and onions to the soup, stirring constantly. Cook over low heat for 30 minutes. Correct seasoning. Add heavy cream, if desired. Serve hot. Makes 6 to 8 servings.

8	small dried mushrooms
¼	c Stone-Buhr pearl barley
8	c water
2	tsp salt
½	tsp freshly ground black pepper
2	tbsp shortening
1	onion, chopped fine
1	tbsp Stone-Buhr all-purpose flour
½	c heavy cream (optional)

CORNY SCALLOP CHOWDER

2 lbs scallops
1 qt water
½ c butter or margarine
2 c sliced onions
2 tbsp Stone-Buhr potato starch
2½ c cubed potatoes
1 c coarsley chopped celery
1 bay leaf
½ tsp MSG or Accent
¼ tsp pepper
4 c milk
1 c sour cream
2 tbsp Stone-Buhr all-purpose flour
1 #303 can whole kernel corn, drained

The potato starch gives this recipe a flavor all of its own. Served with hot, fresh bread, it is a perfect Sunday night supper.

Simmer scallops in 1 quart water for 5 minutes. Strain. Boil broth until reduced to 1⅔ cups. Add potatoes, celery and seasonings. Simmer until potatoes are tender. Saute onions in butter for 5 minutes. Stir in potato starch; add to broth stirring until smooth. Add milk. Mix sour cream with 2 tablespoons flour. Add sour cream, beating until well blended. Add corn and scallops; blend well. Remove bay leaf. Serve sprinkled with paprika if desired. Makes 3½ quarts.

LEEK SOUP

1 c Stone-Buhr pearl barley
7 c water
1 c diced leeks
1½ c diced celery
1 c diced rutabaga
1 c diced carrots
½ c chopped onion
1 garlic clove, chopped
1 tbsp salt
1 tsp Accent or MSG
1 tbsp vinegar
2 tbsp chopped parsley

Barley and leek — a very delicious combination. The vinegar gives a nice bright taste to the soup.

Cook the barley in 7 cups of water. When it is tender, add remaining ingredients, except parsley and cook for 25 minutes longer. Soup will thicken so stir frequently. Serve with chopped parsley. Makes 6 to 8 servings.

SUNFLOWER SOUP

Sunflower seed soup is a delicious way to start any meal. The sunflower seeds have a slightly nutty taste when cooked in the broth.

Place water, bouillon cubes, salt and sunflower seeds in a saucepan. Bring to a boil and add the sliced carrot and all of the green onion except 2 tbsp. Cover and simmer for about 45 minutes. Serve in bowls and sprinkle each serving with some of the remaining green onion. Serves 5-6.

6	c water
3	chicken bouillon cubes
1	tsp salt
1	c Stone-Buhr sunflower seeds
1	sliced carrot
4	chopped green onions, including tops

FARINA SOUP

This is a very mild soup that is a favorite with people who prefer foods that are not highly seasoned.

Melt butter, add farina, flour and brown until golden in color, stirring constantly. Stir into rapidly boiling, salted water or broth and simmer for 20 minutes. Remove from heat, cool slightly, then add egg yolk. Stir well and serve. Serves 4.

3	tbsp butter or margarine
¼	c Stone-Buhr farina
1	tbsp Stone-Buhr flour
1	tsp salt
1	qt boiling water or chicken broth
1	egg yolk

CHUNKY BEEF SOUP

A beef soup that has a nice hearty flavor.

Very slowly brown stew meat in a small amount of shortening. Combine meat, soup bone, water, salt and pepper; cover tightly. Simmer 1 hour. Chill and skim off fat. Add cooked wheat kernels or barley and simmer 30 minutes, adding additional water if soup gets too thick. Add vegetables and cook for 30 minutes more. Parsley may be added for color. Makes 6 to 8 servings.

1	lb beef stew meat
1	lb soup bone
1	tbsp shortening
2	qts water, approximately
4	tsp salt
¼	tsp pepper
1½	c cooked Stone-Buhr wheat kernels
	or ½ c uncooked Stone-Buhr barley
2	c canned tomatoes
1	c diced carrots
½	c chopped onion
½	c chopped celery

BREADS

Peasant Bread p.99

BREADS

Breadmaking dates back to before Christ, in the Persian Gulf where Ur, an ancient city, was located. At first bread is believed to have been unleavened and baked by the sun. The Egyptians, Greeks and Romans slowly improved techniques of breadmaking. In Egypt, the ancient story goes, a careless slave forgot to bake some moistened wheat flour. Left overnight, yeasts from the air settled into the bread and it fermented and expanded. The next morning the master appeared and saw the fermented dough. Not wanting to explain his neglect, the slave hastily baked some of the dough. The resulting leavened bread was so light and so much better than the regular bread, that the slave gained his freedom as well as fame. This 'sour dough starter' was the ancestor of today's leavened breads. When the Christian era began, followers of Jesus prayed for a good harvest and breads were traditional on special days, much as turkey is a tradition in America on Thanksgiving.

When the immigrants made their way to America, they brought their traditional bread recipes along. Corn was more plentiful than wheat and the Indians showed colonists how to prepare cornbread. Techniques of breadmaking were improved and cornbread became a main part of the diet of the settlers. Travel across the continent was common and cornbread became known as journeycake and later johnnycake. Different regions became known for their breadmaking specialties. For example, biscuits were a contribution of the South; New England was known for Boston Brown Breads; and sour-dough breads were an old west treat.

Bread has been the staff of life for thousands of years, and today homemade bread tastes better than ever before due to science. Our modern ovens with automatic control units have made the process of breadmaking more simplified and accurate.

Handling the common, earthy ingredients that go into bread is fun. The aroma of bread baking in a modern kitchen helps to make your house into a home. Breads that are lovingly prepared in time for an evening meal help to create memories that each family member can enjoy. There are a variety of recipes for you to use in this book. For days when your time is limited, there are many varieties of whole grain breads, baked by Oroweat available in your local markets.

VARYING THE GRAINS YOU USE

This chart is a guide for substituting various Stone-Buhr grains for regular oats.
It includes a description of how the variation will affect your product.

substitution for 1 cup regular oats:	product variation
¼ c scotch oats	
¾ c regular oats	More definite texture in things like bread and cookies
½ c rice flakes	
½ c regular oats	Product is more crunchy and crisp
¾ c wheat flakes	
¼ c regular oats	Product is firmer
¼ c 7 grain cereal	
¾ c regular oats	Product will have distinct flavor from the cereal
¼ c bran flakes	
¾ c oatmeal	Product will be softer
1 c quick oats	A little softer
1 c barley flakes	Similar in texture but a little different taste
1 c cereal mates	Product will be a little firmer and have more flavor

BREADMAKING INGREDIENTS

yeast The growth of yeast, a living plant, in a bread dough makes it rise and become light. Compressed yeast (3/5 oz) and active dry yeast (1 package) may be used interchangeably in the recipes in this book.

salt Salt is added to bread to improve its flavor. Salt also regulates yeast growth.

sugar Sugar furnishes food for the yeast. Refrigerator doughs and sweet doughs contain more sugar than regular breads and can be kept for several days under refrigeration before baking. Usually we use granulated sugar, but brown sugar, molasses or honey can also be used.

eggs Eggs add color and flavor, but are often omitted from plain breads.

flour Some wheat flour is needed in all yeast breads as it provides the network for holding the gas bubbles produced by the yeast. Stone-Buhr unbleached all-purpose flour has excellent breadmaking properties. You may make specialty breads using higher proportions of some of the Stone-Buhr novelty flours (i.e. barley, buckwheat, soy) than recommended in these recipes. To do this, substitute Stone-Buhr gluten flour for ½ the all-purpose flour in the recipe. The novelty flour can then be used to replace the other ½ of the all-purpose flour. Add the gluten flour first, then slowly add the novelty flour as you may need less than the recipe calls for. Flour does not need to be sifted before measuring. The amount needed usually varies so add it slowly.

liquid Liquid used to make breads can be milk or water. Fresh, evaporated or reconstituted dry milk all give similar results and can be used in any of these recipes. Water makes bread crustier than milk.

fat Fats make breads tender with a soft crust and improve the keeping quality of bread. French bread has little fat, is crisp and stales rapidly. Sweet rolls have more fat so are tender and stay fresh for a longer time.

   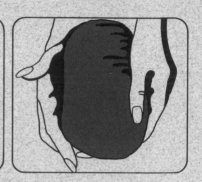

WHITE BREAD

This basic white bread is fun to make. Try substituting a half cup of specialty flours for a change. Each of the specialty flours made by Stone-Buhr has its own unique taste.

Dissolve yeast in warm water. Add remaining ingredients. Mix until dough is formed. Turn out on lightly floured board and knead until smooth and elastic. Round up and place in greased bowl. Grease top and cover with towel. Let rise until double, punch down. Knead and shape into loaf. Place in greased 9 x 5-inch loaf pan. Cover and let rise in pan until double. Bake at 375 degrees about 40 minutes or until done. Remove from pan immediately and cool on wire rack. Makes 1 loaf.

Soy Bread: Use White bread recipe, substituting ¼ cup unsifted Stone-Buhr soy flour and 2¼ cups unsifted Stone-Buhr all-purpose flour. Bake 30 minutes or until done.

Rice Bread: Use White bread recipe, substituting ¼ cup unsifted Stone-Buhr brown rice flour and 2¼ cups unsifted Stone-Buhr all-purpose flour. Bake 30 minutes or until done.

1	pkg active dry yeast
½	c warm water
3	c unsifted Stone-Buhr all-purpose flour
½	c warm milk
1	tbsp sugar
1¼	tsp salt
1	tbsp shortening

GRANDMA'S BREAD

2 pkg active dry yeast
¼ c warm water
2 c milk, scalded
¼ c butter or margarine
½ c sugar
2 tsp salt
2 eggs, beaten
1 c light raisins
6½ c sifted Stone-Buhr all-purpose flour

This is one of my favorite breads because I love light raisins. I like to use it for sandwiches, toasted with butter, or just as it is.

Dissolve yeast in water. Combine milk, butter, sugar and salt; cool to lukewarm. Stir in yeast, eggs, and raisins. Add about 3 cups flour and beat until smooth. Add enough more flour to make dough easy to handle. Turn onto lightly floured board and knead until smooth and elastic. Place dough in a greased bowl; grease top and cover; let rise until double in bulk. Shape into 2 loaves and place in greased pans 9 x 5 x 3-inches. Cover and let rise until double in bulk. Bake at 425 degrees for 40 minutes or until done. Turn out on cake racks to cool. If desired, these loaves may be braided as we did in the picture on the cover. Makes 2 loaves.

50% STONE GROUND WHOLE WHEAT BREAD

1 pkg active dry yeast
¼ c lukewarm water
¼ c sugar
2 tsp salt
2 tbsp shortening
1 c milk
1 c boiling water
2½ c unsifted Stone-Buhr all-purpose flour
3 c unsifted Stone-Buhr 100% stone ground whole wheat flour

This is delicious bread which slices well and is good in sandwiches. Place aluminum foil over top of loaves if they brown too much before they are completely baked.

Dissolve yeast in lukewarm water. In another bowl mix sugar, salt, shortening, milk and boiling water. When milk mixture is lukewarm, add yeast and the 2½ cups all-purpose flour. Slowly start adding the whole wheat flour. When the dough is stiff enough to handle, turn onto a floured board and knead until dough is smooth and elastic. Place in an oiled bowl, cover and let rise until double in bulk. Knead and let rise again. Shape into two loaves; put into greased 9 x 5-inch loaf pans and let rise again until doubled. Bake at 400 degrees for 45 minutes or until golden brown and the loaf sounds hollow when tapped with the fingers. Remove from pan and cool on wire racks. Makes 2 loaves.

FRENCH BREAD

This is about the closest you can get to real French bread. The gluten flour helps give the texture that we enjoy in this type of bread. You must use a pan of water in the oven or the crust will not be crisp enough.

Dissolve yeast in water in large mixing bowl. Add salt, sugar and butter. Stir in gluten flour and enough all-purpose flour to make a soft dough. Turn out on floured pastry cloth. Knead until smooth and elastic, about 10 minutes. Place in a greased bowl. Butter the surface lightly; cover and let rise until double in bulk, about 1 hour. Divide the dough into 3 equal parts. Roll each piece on a lightly floured pastry cloth into a rectangle about 14 x 8 inches. Roll the long side of the rectangle toward you in a tight roll. Pull into shape, about 1½-inches in diameter.

Place seam side down on greased cookie sheets which have been sprinkled lightly with cornmeal. Let rise until double in bulk. Brush with cold water. Sprinkle with salt, if desired. Cut 3 or 4 diagonal slashes across each loaf. Set a shallow pan of water in the bottom of the oven. Bake in a pre-heated 400 degree oven for 50 minutes or until done. Brush loaves with cold water 2 or 3 times while baking. Cool on wire rack. Makes 3 loaves.

1	pkg active dry yeast
2	c lukewarm water
1	tbsp salt
1	tbsp sugar
1	tbsp butter or margarine
1	c unsifted Stone-Buhr gluten flour
4½	c sifted Stone-Buhr all-purpose flour

TWO TONE BREAD

2	pkg active dry yeast
½	c warm water
⅓	c sugar
⅓	c shortening, melted
1	tbsp salt
2½	c milk, scalded and cooled
5¼-5½	c sifted Stone-Buhr all-purpose flour
3	tbsp dark molasses
2¼	c unsifted Stone-Buhr whole wheat flour

This delicious bread is so attractive! The swirl of whole wheat bread throughout the white bread really looks appetizing and tastes delicious.

Dissolve yeast in ½ cup warm water. Add the sugar, shortening, salt and milk. Mix until sugar and salt are dissolved. Add about 3 cups of all-purpose flour and beat well, about 5 minutes. Divide dough in half. To one half, stir in enough of the remaining all-purpose flour to make a moderately stiff dough. Turn onto lightly floured surface and knead till smooth and elastic, 5 to 8 minutes. Place in well-greased bowl, turning once to grease surface; set aside.

To remaining dough, stir in molasses and whole wheat flour. Turn onto lightly floured surface. Knead till smooth and elastic, 5 to 8 minutes, kneading in enough additional all-purpose flour (about 3 tablespoons) to form a moderately stiff dough. Place in well-greased bowl, turning once to grease surface. Cover both doughs and let rise till double in bulk, about 1 to 1¼ hours. Punch down. Cover and let rest on lightly floured surface 10 minutes. Roll out half the light dough and half the dark, each to a 12 x 8-inch rectangle.

Place dark atop light; roll up tightly, beginning at short side. Repeat with remaining doughs. Place in 2 greased 9 x 5-inch loaf pans. Cover and let rise till double in bulk, 45 to 60 minutes. Bake at 375 degrees for 30 to 35 minutes or until done. Remove from pans and cool on wire rack. Makes 2 loaves.

BANANA NUT BREAD

I always make this in miniature loaf pans so that a whole slice is small and easy to handle.

Sift flour once, measure, add baking powder, salt and soda and sift again. Cream shortening, add sugar gradually and cream together until light and fluffy. Add eggs and beat well. Stir in nuts and orange rind. Add flour alternately with bananas, a third at a time, beating after each addition only until smooth. Bake in greased 9x5 inch loaf pan in a moderate oven (350 degrees) for 55 minutes or until done. If you use smaller pans, be sure to decrease the baking time. Store 6 hours or overnight before using. Makes 1 loaf.

1¾	c sifted Stone-Buhr all-purpose flour
2	tsp baking powder
¾	tsp salt
½	tsp soda
⅓	c shortening
½	c firmly packed light brown sugar
2	eggs
½	c coarsely chopped pecans or walnuts (optional)
1	tsp grated orange rind
1	c mashed bananas (2 large)

SWISS OATMEAL BREAD

The Swiss cheese gives this bread a unique taste. It's great toasted.

Scald milk. Stir in brown sugar, salt, and margarine. Cool to lukewarm. Measure warm water into large warm bowl. Sprinkle or crumble in yeast, stir until dissolved. Stir in lukewarm milk mixture, rolled oats, Swiss cheese, and half the flour. Beat until thoroughly blended. Stir in enough flour to make soft dough. Turn out onto lightly floured board and knead until smooth and elastic, about 10 minutes. Place in greased bowl, turning to grease top. Cover, let rise in warm place free from drafts, until double in bulk, about 1 hour. Punch dough down. Turn out onto lightly floured board. Divide dough in half and shape into loaves. Place in 2 greased 9 x 5 x 3-inch loaf pans. Cover, let rise in warm place, free from draft, until double in bulk, about 1 hour. Bake at 375 degrees about 35 minutes or until done. Remove from pans and cool on wire rack. Makes 2 loaves.

1½	c milk
¼	c firmly packed dark brown sugar
2	tsp salt
3	tbsp butter or margarine
½	c warm water
2	pkg active dry or cake yeast
2	c uncooked regular Stone-Buhr rolled oats
1	c grated Swiss cheese
4	c unsifted Stone-Buhr all-purpose flour (approx.)

HIGH PROTEIN BREAD

1 pkg active dry yeast
¼ c warm water
5 c unsifted Stone-Buhr all-purpose flour
½ c nonfat dry milk solids
⅓ c unsifted Stone-Buhr soy flour
¼ c Stone-Buhr wheat germ
¼ c sugar
1 tbsp salt
1 tbsp melted shortening
1¾ c water

A well-known recipe for bread containing soy and wheat germ. This bread slices very nicely.

Dissolve yeast in ¼ cup warm water. Combine dry ingredients in mixing bowl. Add dissolved yeast, melted shortening, and 1¾ cups water, mixing to blend well. Knead dough until smooth and satiny. Place in well-greased bowl. Cover and allow to rise in a warm place for about 1½ hours. Punch down by plunging fist in center of dough. Fold over edges of dough and turn the whole mass upside down. Cover and allow to rise again for 15 to 20 minutes. Shape into 2 loaves; place in greased 9 x 5-inch loaf pans. Cover and allow to stand about 1 hour in a warm place, or until dough rises and fills pans. Bake at 400 degrees for 45 minutes or until done. Remove from pans and cool on wire rack. Makes 2 loaves.

BUCKWHEAT BREAD

2 pkg active dry yeast
1½ c warm water
1 c undiluted evaporated milk
½ c honey
2½ tsp salt
2 tbsp melted shortening
3 c unsifted Stone-Buhr all-purpose flour
1 c unsifted Stone-Buhr buckwheat flour
1 egg, beaten

A yeast bread with a new twist. The buckwheat flour in this recipe lends a distinctive flavor and color.

Soften yeast in ½ cup warm water. Blend in remaining water, evaporated milk, honey, salt and shortening. Gradually stir in 3 cups all-purpose flour. Beat 4 minutes at high speed with electric mixer. Cover and let rise 20 minutes. Stir in buckwheat flour. Stir in additional all-purpose flour to make stiff dough. Cover and let rise 1 to 1½ hours. Stir down and knead till smooth and elastic. Form two loaves, cover and let double in bulk (about 35 minutes). Brush with beaten egg. Bake at 350 degrees for 35 to 40 minutes or until done. Remove from pans and cool on wire rack. Makes 2 loaves.

GLUTEN BREAD

This bread is very low in starch. It has a nice chewy texture and is easy to knead.

Sprinkle dry yeast over the warm water and let stand 10 minutes. Beat in the 2 cups of gluten flour and allow the sponge to rise in a warm place until light and foamy. Combine egg, melted shortening, salt and sugar, then stir into the sponge. Stir in 4 cups of gluten flour, using only enough flour to make a dough that will knead well. Knead and shape into a loaf. Put into greased 9 x 5-inch loaf pan and let rise until double in bulk. Bake at 400 degrees for about 45 minutes or until the loaf sounds hollow. Remove from pan and cool on wire rack. Makes 2 loaves.

3	c warm water
1	pkg active dry yeast
2	c unsifted Stone-Buhr gluten flour
1	egg, beaten
2	tbsp melted shortening
½	tsp salt
2	tbsp sugar
4	c unsifted Stone-Buhr gluten flour (approx.)

OAT BREAD

This is one of my favorite bread recipes. The Scotch oats give this bread such a nice texture. Try this recipe the first chance you get.

Combine Scotch oats, molasses, shortening and salt. Pour over this mixture 2 cups boiling water. Stir in 2 cups sifted flour. Let cool. While cooling, dissolve yeast in ¼ cup warm water. After standing 10 minutes, add yeast to oats mixture. Work in enough sifted flour to be able to handle dough. Turn onto lightly floured board and knead until smooth and elastic. Cover and let rise until double in bulk. Punch down, shape into loaves, and place in a greased 9 x 5 x 3-inch loaf pan. Let rise again until double. Bake at 375 degrees, 40 minutes or until done. Remove from pan and cool on wire rack. Makes 1 loaf.

1	c Stone-Buhr Scotch oats
¼	c dark molasses
1	tbsp shortening
1	tsp salt
2	c boiling water
4	c sifted Stone-Buhr all-purpose flour, approximately
1	pkg active dry yeast
¼	c warm water

100% STONE GROUND WHOLE WHEAT BREAD

1 pkg active dry yeast
1½ c lukewarm water
1½ c milk
2 tsp salt
3 tbsp brown sugar
3 tbsp shortening
5 c unsifted Stone-Buhr 100% stone ground whole wheat flour

This bread takes an unusually long time to rise because it is made from all whole wheat flour. It is tasty and well worth waiting for.

Dissolve yeast in lukewarm water. Scald milk and pour in a large bowl. Add salt, brown sugar and shortening to the scalded milk. Stir until sugar dissolves. When milk mixture has cooled to lukewarm, add the yeast mixture. Gradually add whole wheat flour. When the dough is stiff enough to handle (about 4 cups flour), turn it out onto a floured board and knead thoroughly, gradually adding as much of the rest of the flour as necessary. Try to keep the dough soft by kneading in only enough flour to keep it from sticking.

Place in a well greased bowl and let rise for about 2 to 3 hours or until doubled. Punch down and shape into 2 loaves. Place in greased 9 x 5-inch loaf pans and allow to rise until almost doubled, about 2 hours, still keeping dough warm. Bake at 325 degrees for 1½ hours, or until loaves sound hollow when tapped with the fingers. Remove from pan and cool on wire rack. Makes 2 loaves.

CARDAMOM BRAID

Cardamom is the second most expensive spice in the world. It is the seed of the ginger plant and must be snipped from the plant by hand. It is delicious in pastries and is a favorite in Scandinavian countries.

Dissolve yeast in ½ cup of warm milk. Cream the butter and sugar. Beat in the egg. Then add yeast mixture, remaining milk, salt and cardamom. Gradually mix in the flour to make a moderately soft dough. Turn out onto lightly floured surface; knead till smooth and elastic, 5 to 8 minutes. Place in lightly greased bowl, turning once to grease surface. Cover; let rise till dough has doubled, about 1¼ hours. Punch down. Turn out onto lightly floured surface and divide dough in ⅓'s; form into balls. Let rest 10 minutes.

Roll each ball to a 16-inch long rope. Line up the 3 ropes, 1 inch apart, on greased baking sheet. Braid loosely, beginning in the middle and working towards the ends. Pinch ends together and tuck under. Cover; let rise about 40 minutes, till almost double. Brush with a little milk. Sprinkle with 1 tablespoon sugar. Bake in a 375 degree oven for 20 to 25 minutes or until nicely browned. Cool on wire rack. Makes 1 braid.

1	pkg active dry yeast
¾	c milk
¼	c butter or margarine
⅓	c sugar
1	egg
½	tsp salt
¾	tsp ground cardamom
2¾ to 3	c sifted Stone-Buhr all-purpose flour

HONEYED WHEAT

2 pkg active dry yeast
½ c lukewarm water
¼ c honey
3 tbsp shortening
1 tbsp grated lemon peel
2¼ c water
3¼-4¼ c unsifted Stone-Buhr
all-purpose flour
1 tbsp salt
2 c unsifted Stone-Buhr whole
wheat flour
Salad oil to grease pans

This recipe is a variation of whole wheat bread that I like because the flavor is so distinct yet not overpowering.

In ½ cup of lukewarm water, dissolve yeast. Combine honey, shortening and lemon peel. Add dissolved yeast and remainder of water. Combine 2 cups all-purpose flour and salt, stirring well to blend. Add to yeast mixture. Add 1 cup whole wheat flour. Beat until thick and elastic. Stir in remaining 1 cup whole wheat flour. Then gradually stir in just enough remaining all-purpose flour to make a soft dough that leaves the sides of bowl.

Turn onto floured board; round up into a ball. Knead 5 to 10 minutes, or until dough is smooth and elastic. Cover and let rise until doubled. Punch down and shape into 2 loaves. Place in greased 9 x 5-inch loaf pans. Let rise until doubled. Bake at 400 degrees for 30 to 40 minutes or until done. Remove from pans immediately. Brush top crust with shortening after baking if you want a soft crust. Makes 2 loaves.

WHOLE WHEAT BREAD

1 pkg active dry yeast
¾ c warm water
1 c warm milk
⅓ c molasses
2 tbsp shortening
2 tsp salt
4 c unsifted Stone-Buhr whole wheat
flour (approximately)

Because this bread uses all whole wheat flour, it will take almost twice as long to rise. Just be patient and you will have a delightful bread. The dough will be a little tacky and not as smooth as breads with white flour.

Dissolve yeast in warm water. Add milk, molasses, shortening and salt. Mix in enough whole wheat flour to make a soft dough. Knead until smooth. Place in greased bowl, cover and let rise until doubled. Punch down and shape into a loaf; place in greased 9 x 5-inch loaf pan. Cover and let rise until double in bulk. Bake at 375 degrees for 40 minutes or until done. Remove from pan and cool on wire rack. Makes 1 loaf.

ONION BAGELS

Bagels take a little more handling as they must be simmered in water. These have a strong onion flavor and are delicious toasted and spread with butter or cream cheese.

Stir together 2 cups flour, yeast, sugar, soup mix, and salt. Add water and oil to flour mixture and beat until smooth, about 2 minutes on medium speed of electric mixer or 300 strokes by hand.

Blend in eggs, 1 at a time. Add 1 cup flour and beat 1 minute on medium speed or 150 strokes by hand. Stir in enough more flour to make a moderately stiff dough. Turn onto lightly floured surface and knead 2 minutes. Shape into ball and place in lightly greased bowl, turning to grease all sides. Cover; let rise in warm place (80 to 85 degrees) until doubled, about 1½ hours. Punch down and let rise again in warm place until doubled, about 45 minutes. Punch down; turn onto lightly floured surface and knead until smooth and satiny, about 8 to 10 minutes. Divide dough into 18 equal portions; roll each into 11-inch strip about ¾ inch in diameter. Seal ends of strip securely with water to make 16 rings.

Place on lightly floured baking sheet. Broil about 1½ minutes on each side or until lightly browned. Drop bagels into gently boiling water; simmer 4 to 5 minutes. Remove from water and drain. Place on lightly greased baking sheet and bake at 350 degrees for 45 to 55 minutes or until done. Makes 18 bagels.

5-6	c unsifted Stone-Buhr all-purpose flour
2	pkg active dry yeast
¼	c sugar
1	pkg (1⅜ oz) dry onion soup mix
2	tsp salt
1⅓	c warm water
⅓	c oil
2	eggs
	Boiling water

BRIOCHE

1 c milk
½ c butter or margarine
1 tsp salt
½ c sugar
2 pkg active dry yeast
¼ c warm water (110-115 degrees)
4 eggs, beaten
1 tsp grated lemon peel
5 c sifted Stone-Buhr all-purpose flour (approx.)
Melted butter

These rich rolls take time to prepare, but are delicious. They can be shaped however you would like, but I have given you instructions for the traditional shape.

Scald milk; stir in butter, salt and sugar. Cool to lukewarm. Sprinkle yeast on warm water; stir to dissolve. Combine eggs and lemon peel and add with yeast to milk mixture. Beat in flour, a little at a time, to make a soft dough you can handle. Turn onto floured board; knead lightly until dough is smooth and satiny. Place in greased bowl; turn dough over to grease top. Cover and let rise in warm place free from drafts until doubled, about 2 hours. Punch down and turn out on floured board. Knead lightly. Shape ⅔ of dough into smooth balls about 2 inches in diameter. Shape remaining dough In 1-Inch balls.

Place large balls in greased muffin pan cups. Flatten balls slightly; make a deep indentation in each with finger or the handle of a wooden spoon. Shape small balls like teardrops and set one firmly in the indentation of each ball in muffin pan cups. Brush with melted butter. Cover and let rise until doubled, about 1 hour. Bake in hot oven (425 degrees) about 10 minutes. Remove from pans at once. Place on wire racks. Serve warm. Makes 3 dozen rolls.

REFRIGERATOR WHOLE WHEAT ROLLS

This dough will keep for about 5 days in the refrigerator. The rolls are delicious and light.

Scald milk; add sugar, salt and shortening. Cool to lukewarm. Sprinkle yeast on warm water; stir to dissolve. Combine milk mixture, 1 cup whole wheat flour and 1 cup all-purpose flour. Beat well with electric mixer for 2 minutes at medium speed or 8 minutes by hand. Scrape bowl occasionally. Add yeast mixture and eggs and beat well. Stir in whole wheat flour and enough all-purpose flour so dough leaves sides of bowl. Place in greased bowl, turn over to grease top. Store covered in refrigerator. Remove 2 hours before shaping. Turn onto floured board, knead, shape as desired. Place on greased pans. Cover, let rise 1 to 1½ hours in warm place. Bake at 400 degrees for 15 to 20 minutes or until done. Makes 4 dozen rolls.

1¾	c milk
½	c sugar
1	tbsp salt
3	tbsp shortening
2	pkgs active dry yeast
½	c warm water (110 to 115 degrees)
4-4½	c unsifted Stone-Buhr whole wheat flour
3	c sifted Stone-Buhr all-purpose flour
2	eggs, beaten

VERY YELLOW CORNBREAD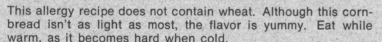

This allergy recipe does not contain wheat. Although this cornbread isn't as light as most, the flavor is yummy. Eat while warm, as it becomes hard when cold.

Stir dry ingredients together. Beat eggs, buttermilk, and lard together. Add dry ingredients and blend thoroughly. Spread in 8 x 8-inch preheated, greased pan. Bake at 425 degrees for 25 minutes, or until done. Cut into squares or wedges and serve hot. Makes 9 servings.

2	c Stone-Buhr cornmeal
½	tsp salt
1	tsp baking powder
½	tsp soda
2	eggs
2	c buttermilk
⅓	c melted lard or shortening

⊙ PEASANT BREAD

2 pkg active dry yeast
½ c warm water
2 c warm water
3 c unsifted Stone-Buhr rye flour
1½ tsp salt
2 tbsp molasses
2 c mashed potatoes
2 tbsp caraway or dill seeds
4 c unsifted Stone-Buhr all purpose flour

Peasant bread has a delicious flavor—try it both ways, once with caraway seeds, again with dill seed.

Dissolve yeast in ½ cup warm water. Add 2 cups water, 2 cups of rye flour, salt, molasses, potatoes, and caraway or dill seed. Blend together. Stir in white flour. Turn out on floured board and knead well, kneading in the remaining cup of rye flour and additional white flour if necessary to make smooth and elastic. (This is a large quantity of dough and may require a bit more kneading than most doughs). Let rise to double in bulk (30 to 40 minutes). Punch down and divide in half. Knead again for 2 to 3 minutes. Shape and place in two 9 x 5-inch loaf pans or two 9-inch rounds or casseroles which have been greased. Allow to rise until double in bulk. Bake 10 minutes at 425 degrees, lower heat to 375 degrees and bake about 30 to 40 minutes or until done. To obtain a softer crust, brush loaves with glaze 10 minutes before end of baking time. *Glaze:* Bring 1 cup water to boiling point. Make paste of 1 tablespoon plus 1 teaspoon cornstarch in ¼ cup cold water. Add to hot water. Bring to boiling point. Brush cornstarch mixture on loaves. Remove from pans and cool on wire rack. Makes 2 loaves.

ONION RYE BREAD

I love onions. They make this bread a little difficult to knead, but they make the bread moist and delicious.

Scald milk and add sugar, salt and oil. Cool mixture to luke-warm. Soften the yeast in water and add to the milk mixture. Add white flour and mix well. Stir in caraway seeds, onion and 2 cups rye flour and mix. Turn onto surface sprinkled with remaining ½ c rye flour and knead until smooth and elastic, adding enough rye flour to give a fairly stiff dough. Place in a greased bowl, grease top, cover with a towel and let stand in a warm place until double in bulk, about 1 hour.

Punch down, cover, and let rise again until double in bulk. Grease three 9 x 5 inch loaf pans and sprinkle with cornmeal. Divide the dough into ⅓'s, shape the loaves and place in pans. Brush the tops with cream and sprinkle with salt. Cover with a towel and let rise in a warm place until double in bulk, about 1 hour. Bake at 350 degrees for 1 hour or until loaves have a hollow sound when tapped. Turn out on rack to cool. Makes 3 loaves.

2	c milk
¼	c sugar
4	tsp salt
¼	c salad oil
1	pkg active dry yeast
1	c lukewarm water
6	c sifted Stone-Buhr all-purpose flour
3	tbsp caraway seeds
1	c chopped onions
2½	c unsifted Stone-Buhr rye flour, approximately
¼	c Stone-Buhr cornmeal
2	tbsp cream

RYE-CORN-WHEAT BREAD

This is a nice combination bread. Let it cool thoroughly and then slice it for sandwiches or toast. You may wish to shape this bread in round loaves and make them on a cookie sheet. That is what we did in the bread divider page.

Dissolve yeast in milk. Add the remaining ingredients and mix thoroughly. Let rise in a warm place until double in bulk. Knead down and shape into 2 loaves. Place in 2 greased 9 x 5-inch loaf pans. Let rise again until double in bulk. Bake in a 350 degree oven for about 40 minutes or until done. Remove from pans and cool on wire rack. Makes 2 loaves.

1	pkg active dry or cake yeast
2	c lukewarm milk
½	c light molasses
1	tsp salt
1	c unsifted Stone-Buhr rye flour
1	c Stone-Buhr cornmeal
3	c sifted Stone-Buhr all-purpose flour
2	tbsp melted shortening

BARLEY FLAKE BREAD

¾ c boiling water
½ c Stone-Buhr barley flakes
3 tbsp shortening
¼ c light molasses
2 tsp salt
1 pkg active dry yeast
¼ c warm water (110-115 degrees)
1 egg, beaten
2¾ c sifted Stone-Buhr all-purpose flour

An interesting white bread with barley flakes and molasses. This batter bread does not have to be kneaded or shaped.

Stir together boiling water, barley flakes, shortening, molasses and salt. Cool to lukewarm. Sprinkle yeast on warm water; stir to dissolve. Add yeast, egg, and 1¼ cup flour to barley flake mixture. Beat with an electric mixer at medium speed for 2 minutes. With a spoon, beat and stir in remaining flour until batter is smooth.

Grease 9 x 5-inch loaf pan and sprinkle with a little barley flakes and salt. Spread batter in pan. With a floured hand, gently smooth top and shape loaf. Cover and let rise until batter just reaches the top of the pan, about 1½ hours. Bake at 375 degrees for 25 to 35 minutes or until done. Remove from pan and cool on rack before slicing. Makes 1 loaf.

HONEY RYE BREAD

1 pkg. active dry yeast
½ c warm water
1 c Stone Buhr rye flakes
1 c Stone Buhr whole wheat flour
½ c honey
¼ c corn syrup
¼ c shortening
2 tsp salt
2 c boiling water
6-7 c Stone Buhr all purpose flour
1 egg

This braided loaf is slightly sweet and tastes delicious when spread with cream cheese.

Dissolve the yeast in ½ c warm water. Place the rye flakes, whole wheat flour, honey, corn syrup, shortening and salt in a large bowl. Add boiling water and mix well. Cool to lukewarm and add softened yeast. Add enough all purpose flour to make a soft dough. Knead dough until smooth and satiny, about 10 minutes. Grease lightly and place in a bowl. Cover the dough and let rise in a warm place until double, about 1½ hours. Punch down and shape into 3 round loaves. Place on a greased cookie sheet. Cover and let rise until double, about 1 hour. Brush with lightly beaten egg. Bake at 350 degrees for about 30-40 minutes or until the bread sounds hollow when tapped. Remove from cookie sheets and cool on wire racks.

HEIDELBERG RYE BREAD

This rye bread is unusual because it has cocoa in it. I think you'll like the flavor it gives.

Combine 2 cups of all-purpose flour, undissolved yeast, cocoa, sugar, salt and caraway seeds in large bowl. Stir well to blend. Add molasses and shortening. Add hot tap water to ingredients in bowl all at once. Beat with electric mixer at medium speed for 2 minutes. Scrape bowl occasionally. Add remaining all-purpose flour. Beat with electric mixer at high speed 1 minute or until thick. By hand, gradually stir in enough rye flour to make a soft dough that leaves the sides of the bowl. Turn onto a floured board and knead 5 to 10 minutes, or until smooth. Cover dough well and let rest 20 minutes, then punch down and divide in half.

Shape each portion into a round loaf. Place in greased 8-inch pie pans. Brush surface of dough with oil. Cover loosely with plastic wrap. Refrigerate 2 to 24 hours. When ready to bake, remove from refrigerator, uncover and let stand 10 minutes. Slash an X in top of each loaf. Bake at 400 degrees for 30 to 35 minutes, or until done. Remove from pans immediately. Cool on racks. Makes 2 loaves.

3	c unsifted Stone-Buhr all-purpose flour
2	pkg active dry yeast
¼	c cocoa
1	tbsp sugar
1	tbsp salt
1	tbsp caraway seeds
⅓	c molasses
2	tbsp shortening
2	c hot tap water
2½-3½	c unsifted Stone-Buhr rye flour
	Salad oil

RUSSIAN BLACK BREAD

2½	c warm water (115 degrees)
2	pkg active dry yeast
1	tsp sugar
2	tsp salt
¼	c butter or margarine softened
¼	c dark molasses
¼	c vinegar
1	sq (1 oz) unsweetened chocolate, melted
2	tbsp caraway seeds, crushed
2	tsp instant coffee
2	tsp onion powder or flakes
½	tsp fennel seeds, crushed
2	c Stone-Buhr bran flakes
4	c unsifted Stone-Buhr rye flour
3¼	c unsifted Stone-Buhr all-purpose flour (approx.)
1	tsp cornstarch
½	c cold water

This bread is delicious. It gets its black color from the rye flour, molasses, coffee and chocolate.

Measure warm water into large bowl. Sprinkle yeast into water and stir until dissolved. Stir in sugar, salt, margarine, molasses, vinegar, chocolate, caraway seeds, instant coffee, onion powder, fennel seeds, bran flakes and rye flour. Beat until thoroughly blended. Stir in enough white flour to make a stiff dough. Transfer dough onto lightly floured board. Knead until smooth and elastic, about 10 minutes (dough may be sticky).

Form into a smooth ball. Place large bowl upside down over dough and let rest for 15 minutes. Then place dough into greased bowl, turning dough to grease top. Cover and let rise in warm place, free from draft, until double in bulk, about 1 hour. Punch down dough and turn onto lightly floured board. Divide dough in half and shape each half into a ball about 5 inches in diameter. Place each ball in the center of a greased 8-inch layer cake pan and cover. Let rise in warm place, free from draft, until double in bulk, about 1 hour.

Bake in 350 degree oven about 45 minutes or until done. Meanwhile, mix together the cornstarch and cold water. Cook over medium heat, stirring constantly for 1 minute. As soon as bread is baked, brush cornstarch mixture over top of loaves. Return bread to oven and bake 2 or 3 minutes longer, until glaze is set. Remove from pans. Let cool on wire racks away from drafts. Makes 2 round loaves, about 2 pounds each.

WHEAT GERM CASSEROLE BREAD

This bread has a good flavor and is a good recipe for a beginning breadmaker. It is a batter bread, which means it doesn't have to be kneaded or shaped.

Mix 1 cup flour, salt, wheat germ and yeast. Add shortening; gradually add hot water and molasses and beat at medium speed with electric mixer until smooth. Add ½ cup flour, beat 2 more minutes. Stir in enough of remaining flour to make a stiff batter. Cover, let rise in warm place until double in bulk (about 45 minutes). Stir down and beat vigorously, about ½ minute. Turn into greased 1½ quart round casserole. Bake at 375 degrees 45 minutes or until done. Remove immediately from casserole. Makes 1 loaf.

2¾-3¼	c unsifted Stone-Buhr all-purpose flour
2	tsp salt
½	c Stone-Buhr wheat germ
2	pkg active dry yeast
2	tbsp shortening
1⅓	c very hot water
2	tbsp molasses

ANNADAMA BATTER BREAD

This is an old recipe that got its name from a fisherman's wife named Anna. Because she was lazy and he had to bake the bread, he called it Annadama bread.

Stir together boiling water, cornmeal, shortening, molasses and salt. Cool to lukewarm. Sprinkle yeast on warm water; stir to dissolve. Add yeast, egg, and 1¼ cups flour to cornmeal mixture. Beat with an electric mixer at medium speed for 2 minutes. With a spoon, beat and stir in remaining flour until batter is smooth. Grease 9 x 5-inch loaf pan and sprinkle with a little cornmeal and salt. Spread batter in pan. With a floured hand, gently smooth top and shape loaf. Cover and let rise until batter just reaches the top of the pan, about 1½ hours. Bake at 375 degrees for 25 to 35 minutes or until done. Remove from pan and cool on rack before serving. Makes 1 loaf.

¾	c boiling water
½	c Stone-Buhr yellow cornmeal
3	tbsp shortening
¼	c light molasses
2	tsp salt
1	pkg dry yeast
¼	c warm water (110-115 degrees)
1	egg, beaten
2¾	c sifted Stone-Buhr all-purpose flour

KUCHEN DOUGH

1	pkg active dry yeast
¼	c warm water
¾	c scalded milk
⅓	c shortening
¼	c sugar
1	tsp salt
2	eggs, beaten
½	tsp vanilla
3½	c unsifted Stone-Buhr all-purpose flour (approx.)

This is a basic dough that you can use to make cinnamon rolls, pecan rolls, coffee cakes and the like. Use your favorite recipe for a filling. This dough will keep for 3 days if well covered and in there frigerator. This foundation dough can be used for all yeast raised coffee cakes.

Dissolve yeast in water. Pour milk over shortening, sugar and salt. When shortening is completely melted, add eggs and vanilla. Cool to lukewarm and stir in dissolved yeast. Mix well, add flour gradually, beating until dough is smooth and too stiff to beat with spoon. Do not use more than 3 cups of flour while dough is in the bowl. Turn out onto lightly floured board and knead until smooth, about 8 minutes. Place kneaded dough in a well greased bowl, cover, and let double in size. Turn out on very lightly floured board and knead one minute. Shape as desired.

Let rise again until double, about 1 hour. Bake at 350 degrees until done, about 1 hour, depending on shape of the coffee cake; 15 to 20 minutes for sweet rolls. Full recipe of dough will make one very large coffee cake, or 1½-2 dozen sweet rolls.

DILLY CASSEROLE BREAD

This batter bread uses cottage cheese and dill seed to make it flavorful. Try it with fried chicken.

Sprinkle yeast over warm water; stir to dissolve. Heat cottage cheese to lukewarm; combine in mixing bowl with sugar, onion, butter, dill seeds, salt, soda, egg and yeast. Add flour a little at a time, to make a stiff batter, beating well after each addition. Cover and let rise in warm place until doubled, 50 to 60 minutes. Stir down with 25 vigorous strokes. Turn into well-greased, 1½ quart, round casserole. Cover and let rise in warm place 30 to 40 minutes or until almost doubled. Bake in a 350 degree oven for 40 to 50 minutes, until bread is a rich brown color and sounds hollow when tapped lightly with the fingers. Cover with foil the last 15 minutes to prevent excessive browning, if necessary. Remove from pan and cool on wire rack. Makes 1 loaf.

1	pkg active dry yeast
¼	c warm water (110-115 degrees)
1	c large curd creamed cottage cheese
2	tbsp sugar
1	tbsp instant minced onion
1	tbsp butter or margarine
2	tsp dill seeds
1	tsp salt
¼	tsp soda
1	egg, beaten
2¼-2½	c sifted Stone-Buhr all-purpose flour

LEMON POPPY SEED BREAD

Slice this bread, spread with butter and serve with other tea breads.

Combine poppy seeds and milk; set aside. Sift dry ingredients. Cream shortening and gradually add sugar. Add eggs one at a time, beating well after each. Add dry ingredients alternately with milk mixture. Stir in lemon rind. Pour into greased 9 x 5-inch loaf pan. Bake at 350 degrees for 45 to 50 minutes or until done. Remove from pan and cool on wire rack. Makes 1 loaf.

1	tbsp poppy seeds
½	c milk
2	c sifted Stone-Buhr all-purpose flour
1	tbsp baking powder
1	tsp salt
1	c shortening
¾	c sugar
2	eggs
1	tbsp grated lemon rind

PUMPKIN BREAD

1½ c sugar
½ c oil
2 eggs, beaten
1 c pumpkin
⅓ c water
1¼ c unsifted Stone-Buhr all-purpose flour
¾ c unsifted Stone-Buhr whole wheat flour
1 tsp soda
1 tsp salt
½ tsp allspice
½ tsp cinnamon
½ tsp cloves
½ tsp nutmeg
¼ tsp baking powder
½ c raisins

This bread slices easier if allowed to cool thoroughly. It is delicious and makes a nice variation when served with a tray of nut breads.

Mix sugar and oil. Add eggs, pumpkin and water. Sift dry ingredients together; add to pumpkin mixture. Blend well. Stir in raisins. Pour into greased 9 x 5-inch loaf pan. Bake 350 degrees for 1 hour or until done. Remove from pan and cool on wire rack. Makes 1 loaf.

BANANA FRUIT BREAD

⅓ c butter or margarine
⅔ c sugar
2 eggs
1 c mashed bananas
¼ c buttermilk or sour milk
1¼ c sifted Stone-Buhr all-purpose flour
1 tsp baking powder
½ tsp salt
½ tsp baking soda
1 c Stone-Buhr bran flakes
¾ c finely cut dried apricots
½ c chopped walnuts

Cut the apricots for this recipe with a pair of kitchen shears. You can also add ½ cup candied cherries if you'd like.

Cream butter and sugar. Add eggs and beat well. Mix bananas and milk. Mix dry ingredients, fruit and nuts together; add alternately with banana mixture to the creamed butter mixture, sugar and eggs. Pour into greased 9 x 5-inch loaf pan. Bake at 350 degrees for 1 hour, or until done. Makes 1 loaf.

CORNBREAD

This can be baked as muffins or corn sticks. Use as a base for creamed fish or poultry.

Combine cornmeal with remaining dry ingredients. Add sour milk and egg. Blend, stir in oil. Pour into greased 8-inch square pan, muffin or heated cornstick pans. Bake at 350 degrees for 30 minutes or until done. Makes 9 servings.

¾	c Stone-Buhr yellow cornmeal
1	c sifted Stone-Buhr all-purpose flour
1	tsp baking powder
2	tbsp sugar
½	tsp salt
¼	tsp soda
¾	c sour milk
1	egg, beaten
2	tbsp oil

TOPPER CORNBREAD

A cheesy corn bread with a touch of pizza flavor. You can use more onion if you prefer.

Combine cornmeal with remaining dry ingredients. Add sour milk and egg. Blend. Stir in oil. Pour into greased 8-inch square pan. Cook onion in butter till tender, but not brown, on low heat. Sprinkle cheese evenly over batter; dot onion butter mixture over all; sprinkle with celery seed. Bake at 375 degrees 20 minutes or until done. Cut into squares or wedges. Makes 9 servings.

¾	c Stone-Buhr yellow cornmeal
1	c sifted Stone-Buhr all-purpose flour
1	tsp baking powder
2	tbsp sugar
½	tsp salt
¼	tsp soda
¾	c sour milk
1	egg, beaten
2	tbsp oil

Topping:

¼	c chopped onion
1	tbsp butter or margarine
1	c shredded cheddar cheese
1	tsp celery seed

FIESTA CORNBREAD

1½ c unsifted Stone-Buhr all-purpose flour
2 tbsp baking powder
1 tsp salt
¼ c sugar
1½ c Stone-Buhr yellow cornmeal
⅓ c grated Parmesan cheese
¼ c chopped green peppers
¼ c finely sliced green onions
6 tbsp melted butter or margarine
4 tsp chili powder
1⅓ c milk
2 eggs, slightly beaten

If you have any cornbread left, toast it and serve it with eggs for breakfast.

Sift together the flour, baking powder, salt and sugar; stir in cornmeal, Parmesan cheese, green pepper and onion. Combine the butter and the chili powder; stir in milk and then eggs. Pour milk mixture all at once into dry ingredients and stir just until blended. Turn batter into a well-greased, 9-inch square baking pan or a 10-inch heavy frying pan. Bake in a 400 degree oven for about 35 minutes, or until a pick inserted into the center comes out clean. Cut in squares or wedges and serve hot. Makes 8 to 10 servings.

WHOLE WHEAT BISCUITS

1 c sifted Stone-Buhr all-purpose flour
1 tsp baking powder
1 tsp salt
1 c unsifted Stone-Buhr whole wheat flour
¼ c lard or shortening
¾ c milk (approximately)

These whole wheat biscuits are light and flaky and have a delicious whole wheat flavor.

Sift together the all-purpose flour, baking powder and salt. Add the whole wheat flour and stir to mix well. Cut in lard until mixture resembles coarse meal or crumbs. Make a hollow in flour-shortening mixture and stir in enough milk to make a soft dough that leaves the sides of the bowl and sticks to the mixing fork. Turn onto lightly floured surface and knead with heal of hand 15 times. Roll ¼ to ½-inch thick. Cut with 2-inch cutter; lift cutouts to ungreased baking sheet with broad spatula. Place close together for soft sides, 1-inch apart for crusty sides. Bake 450 degrees 10 to 12 minutes, or until golden brown. Serve at once. Makes 12 to 16 biscuits.

SPICED APPLE MUFFINS

Wheat germ gives these biscuits a delicious flavor. Serve them hot with honey or home-made jam.

Combine flour, wheat germ, baking powder and salt in mixing bowl. Stir to blend thoroughly. Cut in shortening with pastry blender until mixture looks like coarse cornmeal. Add milk all at once and stir with a fork just until all ingredients are moistened. Turn onto floured board and knead lightly 15 to 20 times. Roll dough ½-inch thick. Cut with 2-inch floured cutter. Place on ungreased baking sheet. Bake at 450 degrees for 12 to 15 minutes or until golden brown. Makes 12 biscuits.

1½	c sifted Stone-Buhr all-purpose flour
½	c Stone-Buhr wheat germ
1	tbsp baking powder
1	tsp salt
¼	c shortening
¾	c milk

HERB BISCUITS

You should experiment with other herbs besides the ones in this recipe. I like to serve these with stews or roast beef.

Sift dry ingredients; add herbs. Cut in shortening. Add liquid and stir to make a soft dough. Knead lightly, roll ½-inch thick. Cut out biscuits and place on an ungreased baking sheet. Bake at 425 degrees for about 10 minutes or until golden brown. Makes 12 biscuits.

2	c sifted Stone-Buhr all-purpose flour
2	tsp baking powder
¼	tsp baking soda
1	tsp salt
¼	tsp dry mustard
½	tsp dry sage
½	tsp celery seed
¼	c butter or margarine
¾	c buttermilk

CHEESE BISCUITS

2 c sifted Stone-Buhr all-purpose flour
2 tsp baking powder
¼ tsp soda
1 tsp salt
¼ c butter or margarine
½ c grated dry sharp American cheese
¾ c buttermilk (approximately)

I use sharp cheddar cheese in these biscuits. They are so flavorful and moist that they are delicious just plain.

Sift together dry ingredients. Cut in shortening finely and stir in cheese. Stir in buttermilk to make a soft dough. Knead lightly about 15 times. Roll to ½-inch thick on floured board. Cut and bake on ungreased baking sheet at 425 degrees until golden brown. Makes 12 biscuits.

WHEAT GERM BISCUITS

1 c sifted Stone-Buhr all-purpose flour
1 tsp baking powder
1 tbsp sugar
½ tsp salt
1 egg, well beaten
⅓ c milk
¼ c melted shortening, or salad oil
½ c peeled and chopped apples
Topping:
1 tbsp sugar
⅛ tsp cinnamon

These fruit muffins are fun to serve in the wintertime when fresh berries are unavailable. I like to leave the peel on the apples for added color. If your pan is for 12 muffins, put water in the cups you aren't using.

Measure sifted flour, add baking powder, sugar and salt and sift again. Combine egg and milk and add all at once to flour mixture. Add shortening and apples; stir only until dry ingredients are dampened. (Batter will be lumpy). Spoon into greased muffin pans, filling each ⅔'s full. Before baking, sprinkle tops with a mixture of 1 tablespoon of sugar and dash of cinnamon. Bake at 400 degrees about 25 minutes or until done. Makes 6 muffins.

RICE and
BARLEY FLOUR MUFFINS 🔄

This allergy recipe contains no wheat or eggs. These muffins have a barley flavor and they are nice to serve with roast pork or beef.

Sift dry ingredients together. Add liquid and melted fat. Stir only enough to combine. Fill greased muffin pans ⅔'s full. Bake at 400 degrees for 25 to 35 minutes or until done. Makes 5 muffins.

⅓	c unsifted Stone-Buhr rice flour
⅔	c unsifted Stone-Buhr barley flour
1	tbsp baking powder
2	tbsp sugar
¼	tsp salt
¾	c milk
1	tbsp melted margarine

ORANGE
SUNFLOWER SEED BREAD

Wait until this bread is completely cooled before slicing. For easier slicing, coarsely chop sunflower seeds before adding them.

Sift dry ingredients together. Combine egg, orange juice, peel, milk and butter; add to dry ingredients, mixing well. Stir in sunflower seeds. Pour into greased 9 x 5 x 5-inch loaf pan and bake at 350 degrees about 1 hour, or until done. Cool on rack 15 minutes before removing from pan. Makes 1 loaf.

3	c sifted Stone-Buhr all-purpose flour
1	c sugar
1	tsp salt
3½	tsp baking powder
1	egg, beaten
¾	c orange juice
4	tsp grated orange peel
¾	c milk
¼	c butter or margarine, melted
¾	c roasted Stone-Buhr sunflower seeds (shelled)

JUDGING YOUR BREADS

heavy compact texture You have probably worked too much flour into the dough. Sweet dough especially may seem much too soft and sticky, but as you knead it becomes more elastic. Don't put too much flour on the board and keep the dough slightly on the soft side. Compact texture may also be caused by not letting the dough rise long enough.

fallen center You have allowed too long a rising time for the dough.

coarse texture This is caused by too little kneading, too little flour, too long a rising period or too low a temperature for the rising period.

yeasty flavor This is usually caused by allowing the dough to rise too long.

loaves small and flat You may have killed the yeast by using ingredients that were too warm. The yeast may have been too old or the dough may not have risen long enough.

crumbly bread You probably have not mixed the dough enough or had too cool an oven during baking.

TEMPORARILY OUT?

when you need 1 cup of sugar:

Use: 1 cup packed brown sugar

or

1 cup molasses or honey plus ¼ tsp soda. Decrease liquid in recipe ¼ cup for each cup of molasses or honey used

or

1½ cups maple syrup. Decrease liquid in recipe by ¼ cup for each cup of sugar you are replacing.

when you need 1 cup of honey:

Use: 1 cup molasses. Leave soda out of the recipe and replace each ¼ teaspoon of soda with 1 teaspoon baking powder

or

1 cup sugar plus ¼ cup liquid.

DATE BREAD

This is a delicious recipe for a date bread. It slices better if stored overnight before slicing. Try spreading each slice with cream cheese softened with orange juice.

Place chopped dates in a bowl and sprinkle with baking soda. Heat sherry and pour over dates; cool. Cream shortening and sugar. Add eggs, one at a time and beat well. Add vanilla and cooled date and sherry mixture, mix well. Sift flour with baking powder and salt. Add to creamed mixture and stir until blended. Stir in nuts. Pour into 2 greased 7 x 4-inch loaf pans or 1, 9 x 5-inch loaf pan. Bake at 350 degrees for 50-60 minutes or until done.

1	c chopped dates
1	tsp baking soda
¾	c sherry or white wine
¼	c shortening
1	c sugar
2	eggs
1	tsp vanilla
2	c sifted Stone-Buhr all-purpose flour
1	tsp baking powder
½	tsp salt
½	c chopped walnuts

PIES

Clockwise from left: Cereal Mates Crumb Crust p.120. Deep Dish Apple Pie with Whole Wheat Pastry p.128. Irish Coffee Pie p.125

PIES

Some form of pie baking dates back to the earliest civilization of man. The English were masters in pie making and the pies they made served both as the food and container. Pies made in Elizabethan England contained anything edible, including all kinds of meats, fish, fruits and vegetables.
In America, pie is the number one dessert. America has regional pies such as pumpkin and custard in New England, pecan in the South and apple in the West. No matter where you live, you will find some perfect recipes for delicious pies using foods available from the area. During the settling of Early America, sailors used to pass the many hours at sea dreaming of the pies back home and carving pie-jaggers to take home. These implements of bone, often quite fancy but very precise, were used by New England housewives to cut the lattices for their pies.

Every neighborhood has a few experienced women who are locally famous for their crusts and pies. Some beginners believe that homemakers are born with special talents in baking. No special talent is required for pie baking, but a few general guides will help you along.

- Follow the recipe carefully
- Handle the pastry lightly
- Let pie dough rest at least 5 minutes before rolling
- Roll the dough lightly from the center in all directions to make a circle lifting the rolling pin near the edges to avoid getting it too thin on the edge
- Lift the pastry to the pie pan gently and avoid stretching it
- Gently press the dough to fit the shape of the pan
- If you are preparing a pie shell that needs to be baked before being filled, be sure to prick the bottom and sides of the pastry before placing it in the oven.

All the pies in this section have been tested. Follow the directions carefully and the old phrase, "easy as pie," will come true.

Use your pastry scraps to make decorations for the top of your pie. Take scraps from the top pastry and knead well, adding a little extra flour. Let it stand for a few minutes and then roll. The kneading enables you to roll the dough very thin, making it more pliable and easier to cut delicate flowers and decorations. If desired, brush the entire top crust and the decorations with milk before baking.

PASTRY-PASTE METHOD

If you ever have trouble making pastry, here is the answer. This recipe will give you delightful results every time you use it.

Mix flour and salt in a bowl. Cut in shortening. Blend together ½ cup of this mixture and 5 tablespoons of water. Add this paste to the shortening-flour mixture and mix with a fork until the dough holds together and is shaped into a round flat mass. Divide dough in half and make 2, 9-inch pastry shells. Bake at 425 degrees for 12 to 15 minutes, or until lightly browned.

2¼	c unsifted Stone-Buhr pastry flour
1	tsp salt
¾	c solid vegetable shortening
5	tbsp water

PLAIN PASTRY

1 c Stone-Buhr pastry flour
½ tsp salt
¼ c shortening
3 tbsp cold water, approximately

This standard pastry made with pastry flour will give you a nice, flaky, tender crust. Add water carefully as you may need a little less or a little more than the recipe calls for. You want to be sure that you have enough water added so the dough can be rolled nicely, but too much will make the crust too tough.

Blend flour and salt in a mixing bowl. Cut fat into dry ingredients until fat is cut into pieces the size of rice kernels. Sprinkle water evenly over dry ingredients tossing with a fork until all portions are evenly dampened. Press mixture into a ball. Place ball of dough on lightly floured, cloth-covered board. Roll dough from center outward, keeping pastry as round as possible, about ⅛-inch thick. Arrange in 9-inch pie pan. If pastry shell is to be pre-baked before filling, prick bottom and sides with fork tines. Bake at 450 degrees 12 to 15 minutes, or until lightly browned. Makes 1, 9-inch pie shell.

WHOLE WHEAT PASTRY

1 c Stone-Buhr whole wheat flour
½ tsp salt
⅓ c shortening
2 tbsp cold water, approximately

Whole wheat pastry is a delightful change for pie lovers. You may need to add a little more flour to the board when rolling this out as whole wheat pastry tends to be more sticky than regular pastry. The 100% Stone-Buhr whole wheat pastry flour is finer in texture than regular Stone-Buhr whole wheat flour and is recommended for this reason.

See method for plain pastry. Makes 1-9" pastry shell.

WHEAT PASTRY

I especially like this pastry with fruit pies. The whole wheat flour gives it a nut-like taste and a rich brown color.

See method for plain pastry. Makes 1-9″ pastry shell.

½ c Stone-Buhr all-purpose flour
½ c Stone-Buhr whole wheat flour
½ tsp salt
⅓ c shortening
2 tbsp cold water

COCONUT PIE SHELL

This pie shell is good for the summer months when you don't want to heat up the kitchen with the oven. Try the peanut butter chiffon pie filling in this book with this crust.

Combine all ingredients. Pat into a 9-inch pie pan. Chill and fill. Makes 1, 9-inch pie shell.

1 c shredded coconut
½ c Stone-Buhr wheat germ
1 tbsp honey
1 tbsp oil

BUTTER PASTRY

This rich butter pastry can be used to make tart shells or fruit turnovers.

Mix flour, sugar and salt. Add egg yolk and lemon juice and mix lightly with a fork. Add the butter and work it into the dough with your fingers. Add water, if necessary, and work the dough until it forms a ball. Refrigerate ½ hour. Roll out and use as desired. For tart shells, bake in a 400 degree oven for about 7 minutes or until lightly browned. Makes 6-3 inch tart shells.

1 c Stone Buhr all purpose flour or
  pastry flour
2 tbsp sugar
½ tsp salt
1 egg yolk
1 tbsp lemon juice
6 tbsp butter or margarine
1 tbsp water, approximately

ALMOND CRUST

1	20-oz can sliced peaches
⅔	c sugar
¼	c Stone-Buhr all-purpose flour
2	tbsp butter or margarine
⅛	tsp salt
1	tbsp lemon juice
1	unbaked 8-inch pie shell

This peach pie is easy to make using canned peaches. The open top looks even better when each piece is served with a scoop of vanilla ice cream.

Drain the peaches. Mix the sugar, flour, butter and salt together. Sprinkle ⅓ cup of the mixture in the bottom of the pastry shell. Add peaches and lemon juice to the remaining dry mixture. Mix well and pour into the pie shell. Bake at 375 degrees for about 30 minutes or until the filling is clear and bubbling. Cool and serve topped with a scoop of ice cream. Makes 1 8-inch pie.

BERRY PIE

	Pastry for a 2 crust pie
3	c frozen berries (unsweetened)
	Water
¾	c sugar
2	tbsp quick tapioca
1½	tbsp Stone-Buhr potato starch
1	tbsp lemon juice

If you use fresh berries instead of frozen ones, use 4 cups of fruit instead of 3 and ¼ cup water instead of the drained fruit juice. The amount of sugar you use depends on the sweetness of the berries. Decrease it for sweeter fruit and increase it up to 2 cups for very tart, immature fruit.

Thaw berries. Drain liquid and add enough water to have ½ cup. If more liquid drains off, discard and add an equal amount of berries to the rest of the fruit. Mix the juice, sugar, tapioca and potato starch in a saucepan. Heat rapidly until mixture is very thick and clear. Set aside to cool. Stir in berries and lemon juice. Pour the filling into a pastry-lined 9″ pie pan. Top with a full crust. Cut steam vents and flute edges by rolling the top dough under the bottom dough and pinching to seal. Bake at 400 degrees for about 40 min. or until nicely browned. Serves 6-8.

 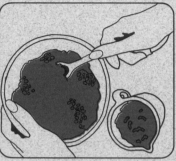  

Crumb crusts are a pastry making short cut because they can be mixed and then just lightly patted into the pan. An easy way to form crusts is to place the crumb mixture in a pie pan, distributing the crumbs fairly evenly.

Then, press another pie pan firmly into the crumbs. Remove the top pan and trim any excess which is forced to the top edge. Crumb crusts such as this cereal mates crust can be pressed into square or oblong pans also. This is especially convenient when the dessert is to be served at potluck or church suppers.

CEREAL MATES CRUMB CRUST

This is really fantastic! Once you prepare a pie with this crust, you'll try to use it with all your favorite recipes.

Heat cereal mates and oats in shallow baking pan at 350 degrees for 10 minutes. Combine cereal, oats, butter and brown sugar, mixing until crumbly. Firmly press into bottom and sides of a 9-inch pie plate. Chill. Fill with favorite chiffon or cream pie filling. Makes 1, 9-inch pie shell.

⅔ c Stone-Buhr cereal mates
⅔ c Stone-Buhr quick oats
⅓ c melted butter or margarine
½ c brown sugar

BASIC FANCY PASTRY

1 c soft butter or margarine
1 c small curd cottage cheese
2 c unsifted Stone-Buhr pastry flour

This pie crust can be stored in the refrigerator for several days before using. Try filling this pastry with any filling you use for tarts. The pastry is crisp and yet very tender.

Beat the butter and cottage cheese together with a mixer until smooth and creamy. Add the pastry flour and beat until thoroughly combined. Roll out half the dough at a time on heavily floured pastry cloth. Fill with a meat or fruit filling.

ORANGE PASTRY

1½ c sifted Stone-Buhr all purpose flour
½ tsp salt
½ c shortening
4-5 tbsp cold orange juice

This pastry is a simple variation of a plain pastry. The orange juice gives the pastry a rich golden color and a nice flavor. Try it with a rhubarb filling.

Mix flour and salt together in a bowl. Cut in shortening until the pieces of fat are the size of small peas. Sprinkle 1 tbsp of orange juice over part of the flour mixture. Gently toss with a fork and push to one side. Repeat until all the flour is moistened. Gather up dough with fingers and form into a ball. Let the dough rest 10 minutes. Roll out on a lightly floured surface until ⅛-inch thick. Transfer pastry to a pie pan and use as directed in the recipe. To make a baked pie shell, flute edges, prick bottom and sides with a fork. Bake at 450 degrees for 10-12 minutes or until nicely browned. Makes one 8-inch pie shell.

hint: Chilling pastry dough after mixing it and before rolling makes pastry easier to handle. I usually refrigerate the dough overnight and then keep it at room temperature one hour before using. Refrigerated dough is easier to roll and does not shrink as much when baked. Always start the baking of a pie crust in an oven that is preheated to correct temperature. This helps create a more tender pastry.

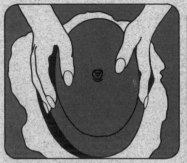   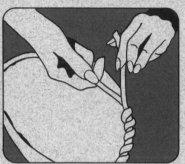

OIL PASTRY CRUST

Oil pastry is especially nice for beginners as it is easy to roll out. This recipe makes a crust that is tender but not as flaky as regular pastry.

Stir flour and salt together. Pour salad oil and cold water together. Add all at once to the flour mixture. Stir lightly with fork. Form in ball with hands. Roll between 2 pieces of waxed paper (about 12″ square). When dough is rolled to edges of paper, peel off the top sheet of paper and place dough, paper side up into pie plate. Remove paper. Trim pie crust to ½″ to 1″ beyond edge. Fold the dough under and flute the edges. For a baked pie shell, prick the bottom and sides and bake at 450 degrees for 12 minutes, or until golden brown. For an unbaked shell, fill with pie filling and bake as directed in the filling recipe. Makes one 8 or 9-inch pie shell. For a double crust pie, make 2 times the recipe.

1	c unsifted Stone-Buhr pastry flour
¾	tsp salt
¼	c salad oil
2½	tbsp cold water

SESAME PECAN PIE

Pastry for a 9-inch pie shell
¼   c Stone-Buhr sesame seeds
3   eggs
¾   c sugar
¼   tsp salt
⅓   c melted margarine or butter
1   c light corn syrup
1½ tsp vanilla
1   c pecan halves

This is a nice variation of pecan pie. The sesame seed flavor is very subtle yet noticeable. Because this is so filling, serve it only after a very light meal.

Line a 9-inch pie plate with pastry. Toast sesame seeds in 350 degree oven for 15 minutes or until golden brown. Sprinkle evenly over bottom of pastry shell. Beat eggs until light and fluffy. Add sugar, salt, butter, corn syrup and vanilla; continue to beat until well mixed. Gently stir in pecan halves. Pour into pastry. Bake in a 350 degree oven for one hour, or until filling is set and pastry is nicely browned. Makes 1, 9-inch pie.

PEANUT BUTTER CHIFFON PIE

¼   c sugar
2   tsp plain gelatin
½   tsp nutmeg
¼   tsp salt
1   c water
½   c peanut butter
2   eggs, separated
1   tsp vanilla
2   tbsp sugar
1   c whipping cream, whipped
1   banana, sliced
1   9-inch Stone-Buhr cereal mates or coconut pie shell

If you like peanut butter as well as I do, this had better be dessert tonight. I like this best when prepared with a cereal mates crumb crust.

Mix ¼ cup sugar, gelatin, nutmeg, and salt. Slowly add water to peanut butter, beating with electric mixer until blended. Combine sugar mixture with peanut butter in top of double boiler. Stir in slightly beaten egg yolks and vanilla. Cook, stirring constantly, until slightly thickened. Chill until partly set. Beat egg whites until foamy; gradually beat in 2 tablespoons sugar. Continue beating until stiff, but not dry. Fold egg whites and half of whipped cream into chilled mixture. Place bananas in pie shell; top with filling. Garnish with remaining whipped cream. Makes 1, 9-inch pie.

CRACKED PECAN PIE

This pie is for all pecan lovers. The filling is very rich, but not as sweet in taste as most pecan pies. I know you'll like it.

Beat eggs. Gradually add oil, brown sugar, maple syrup and milk. Beat well. Add vanilla, salt, cracked wheat and pecans and stir gently. Pour into an unbaked or partially baked (350 degrees for 10 minutes), 9-inch pie shell and bake at 350 degrees for 40 minutes. When the pie is done, remove from the oven and cool on a cake rack until cold before cutting. It may be decorated with whip cream just before serving.

3	eggs
¼	c oil
½	c brown sugar
1	c maple syrup
¾	c milk
1	tsp vanilla
½	tsp salt
¼	c Stone-Buhr cracked wheat
1	c pecans
1	9-inch whole wheat or regular pie shell

COTTAGE CHEESE LIME PIE

This light pie filling is good when prepared with the almond crust or cereal mates pastry. Both pastry recipes are in this book.

The cottage cheese in this recipe makes the filling very creamy without being rich. The blender helps to make the filling smoother, but I like having some texture from small pieces of cottage cheese.

Whirl cottage cheese in a blender or beat with an electric mixer until smooth. In a saucepan, combine gelatin and sugar; stir in milk. Stir over low heat for about 10 minutes. Blend hot mixture into eggs, then stir back into pan; cook 1 minute longer. Remove from heat and mix in cottage cheese, sour cream, lime juice, peel and food coloring. Pour into almond crust. Chill. Makes 8 servings.

1	c large curd cottage cheese
1	pkg unflavored gelatin
¾	c sugar
½	c milk
3	eggs, beaten
1	c sour cream
½	c lime juice
1	tbsp grated lime peel
	Few drops green food coloring
1	almond crumb crust

IRISH COFFEE PIE

1	envelope unflavored gelatin
¾	c sugar
2	tbsp instant coffee powder
1	c milk
2	eggs, separated
1	tbsp sugar
1	tbsp Irish whiskey or ¼ tsp brandy extract
½	pt (1 c) whipping cream
1	9-inch cereal mates pie shell
1	Milk chocolate bar (about ⅓ of 12 oz size), at room temperature

A favorite recipe at the Stone-Buhr Mill kitchens. This dessert is so delicious that once you try it, you'll prepare it often. It takes about 30 minutes in my refrigerator for the gelatin mixture to get like the consistency of egg white.

In a saucepan, blend the gelatin, sugar, and coffee; gradually stir in the milk. Cook over low heat, stirring until the gelatin and sugar are completely dissolved. 5 to 10 minutes. Beat the egg yolks. Stir about half the hot mixture into the yolks. Return all to the pan; cook, stirring constantly, for 3 to 5 minutes, or until slightly thick. Chill until thick and syrupy. Add whiskey to the gelatin mixture and beat until light and frothy.

In another bowl beat egg whites until they form firm but moist peaks; add 1 tbsp sugar; fold into gelatin mixture. Using the same bowl, whip the cream; fold it into the filling. Spread in pie shell. Refrigerate for at least 2 hours or until firm. Garnish with chocolate curls, made by pulling a vegetable peeler firmly across a piece of milk chocolate. Makes 6 to 8 servings.

LEMON MERINGUE PIE

If you use large eggs, you might have some meringue left over from this pie—if so, just fold in some strained apricots or concentrated orange juice. Place in a 350 degree oven and bake until a knife comes out clean. A light fruit whip for a snack.

Combine 1½ c sugar, 1½ c water and salt in a saucepan. Bring to a boil. Mix the cornstarch with ⅓ c water and stir until smooth. Add to the boiling mixture stirring constantly. Cook until thick and clear. Remove from heat. Combine egg yolks and lemon juice; stir into thickened mixture. Return pan to heat and, stirring constantly, heat until mixture again boils. Remove from heat. Stir in lemon peel and butter. Set aside until lukewarm. When the filling is lukewarm, place it in the baked pie shell. Prepare the meringue by beating the egg whites and cream of tartar until frothy. Gradually add ½ c sugar, beating till the egg whites form soft peaks when the beaters are lifted out of the bowl. Pile meringue on top of pie and spread over filling being sure to touch the edge of the pie shell all around the pie. Bake at 350 degrees for about 15 minutes or until lightly browned. Cool and serve. Makes 6-8 servings.

1	9″ baked pie shell
1½	c sugar
1½	c water
½	tsp salt
½	c cornstarch
⅓	c water
4	eggs, separated
½	c lemon juice
1	tsp grated lemon peel
3	tbsp butter or margarine
¼	tsp cream of tartar
½	c sugar

CHERRY PIE

Use any pie crust you like with this cherry pie. You can substitute canned peaches if you like.

Drain cherries and place in mixing bowl. Add ¼ cup of the juice, the sugar, salt and farina. Mix lightly but thoroughly. Line bottom of 8-inch pie pan with pastry. Add cherry mixture. Dot top with butter. Cut thin strips of pastry and arrange on top of pie in lattice design. Bake in hot oven, 400 degrees, until cherries are done, about 1 hour. Cool slightly and serve. Makes 1, 8-inch pie.

1	No. 2 can red sour pitted cherries
¼	c juice
1	c sugar
⅛	tsp salt
2	tbsp Stone-Buhr farina
	Pastry for 8-inch pie
1	tbsp butter or margarine

SHAMROCK LIME PIE

1	9-inch cereal mates pie crust
1	envelope (1 tbsp) plain gelatin
½	c sugar
¼	tsp salt
⅓	c water
⅓	c lime juice
3	eggs, separated
1	tsp grated lemon rind
	Few drops green food coloring
¼	tsp cream of tartar
⅓	c granulated sugar
1	c whipping cream, whipped
	Large green gumdrops

This is nice for Saint Patrick's Day. In the summer leave off the shamrocks and decorate this pie with slices of lemon and fresh mint leaves from the garden.

Combine gelatin, the ½ cup sugar and salt in medium saucepan. Add water and lime juice, blending thoroughly; add egg yolks. Heat to boiling; boil 1 minute, stirring constantly. Remove from heat; stir in lemon rind and food coloring. Chill until mixture is slightly thickened, about the consistency of a fresh egg white.

Beat egg whites until foamy; add cream of tartar and continue beating until stiff peaks form. Gradually add the ⅓ c sugar, beating until sugar is dissolved and meringue is glossy. Fold lime mixture into merinque; fold in whipped cream. Pour into chilled cereal mates crumb pie crust. Chill several hours or until set. Garnish with shamrocks made by rolling out large green gumdrops and cutting with a shamrock-shaped cutter. Makes 1, 9-inch pie.

CARAMEL-RAISIN PIE FILLING

3	eggs
½	c white sugar
1	c brown sugar, packed
¾	c Stone-Buhr rolled oats
2	tbsp margarine or butter
1	tsp vanilla
½	c raisins
	8-inch unbaked pie crust

Try this one! A different and delightful filling for your family and friends.

Beat eggs well in a large bowl. Add white sugar, brown sugar, rolled oats, butter and vanilla. Mix well. Stir in raisins. Pour into unbaked pie crust and bake at 375 degrees for 30 minutes or until firm. Makes 1, 8-inch pie.

DEEP DISH APPLE PIE

This is best if made in an oblong pan. The whole wheat pastry is a nice change with apple filling. Serve it to your family while it is still slightly warm.

Cut margarine finely into whole wheat flour, salt and baking powder. Add beaten egg and water. Mix lightly. Sprinkle ½ c all-purpose flour on board. Lightly knead in enough flour to form a soft dough that can be rolled. Set aside. Toss together apples, sugar, ¼ c all-purpose flour, cinnamon, nutmeg and cloves. Put in buttered 1½ quart shallow baking dish (9x11 is a good size). Sprinkle with water and brandy; dot with margarine.

Roll pastry to about ⅛-inch. Place on top of casserole; trim, leaving ½-inch overhang. Fold under and flute edges. Cut 2 or 3 steam vents in pastry. Sprinkle with cinnamon sugar, if desired. Bake in 425 degree oven 15 minutes. Reduce to 350 degrees and bake 30 minutes longer or until nicely browned. Makes 8 servings.

Pastry:
- ½ c margarine or butter
- 1¼ c Stone-Buhr whole wheat pastry flour
- ¼ tsp salt
- ¼ tsp baking powder
- 1 egg, well beaten
- ¼ c cold water
- ½ c Stone-Buhr all-purpose flour

Filling:
- 6 c sliced tart apples
- ¾ c sugar
- ¼ c Stone-Buhr all-purpose flour
- 1 tsp cinnamon
- ¼ tsp nutmeg
- ¼ tsp cloves
- 1 tbsp water
- 1 tbsp brandy
- 2 tbsp margarine or butter
- Cinnamon sugar, optional

WINTER PEACH PIE

1 20-oz can sliced peaches
⅔ c sugar
¼ c Stone-Buhr all-purpose flour
2 tbsp butter or margarine
⅛ tsp salt
1 tbsp lemon juice
1 unbaked 8-inch pie shell

This peach pie is easy to make using canned peaches. The open top looks even better when each piece is served with a scoop of vanilla ice cream.

Drain the peaches. Mix the sugar, flour, butter and salt together. Sprinkle ⅓ cup of the mixture in the bottom of the pastry shell. Add peaches and lemon juice to the remaining dry mixture. Mix well and pour into the pie shell. Bake at 375 degrees for about 30 minutes or until the filling is clear and bubbling. Cool and serve topped with a scoop of ice cream. Makes 1 8-inch pie.

CUSTARD PIE

1 unbaked 9-inch pie shell
2 c scalded milk
3 large eggs (about ¾ cupful)
¼ tsp salt
⅓ c sugar
½ tsp vanilla
¼ tsp nutmeg

Custard pies should be refrigerated as soon as they cool. If you want to keep the bottom crust crisp, try baking the pie shell for 10 minutes in a 400 degree oven and then add the custard filling and finish baking.

Scald the milk. Mix eggs, salt, sugar and vanilla together. Stir the milk gradually into the egg mixture. Pour into pie shell. Sprinkle with nutmeg. Bake at 400 degrees for 10 minutes. Reduce heat to 350 and bake for 30-40 minutes or until a knife comes out clean when inserted in the center of the custard. Makes 1 9-inch pie.

STRAWBERRY RHUBARB PIE

I love fresh strawberries in rhubarb pie because they have a tart sweetness that is unique. A lattice top is traditional with rhubarb pie and I think it helps to make the filling thicker.

Thoroughly wash and dry rhubarb. Cut into small pieces and measure. If the strawberries are large, cut in half, otherwise leave them whole. Mix sugar, salt and flour together and add to the diced rhubarb and strawberries. Beat the eggs with a fork and add to the rhubarb and strawberry mixture. Fill the unbaked pie shell. Sprinkle with wheat germ and dot with butter. Top the pie with lattice strips and flute the edges of the crust. Bake at 450 degrees for 20 minutes, then reduce heat to 350 degrees and bake about 30 minutes more or until nicely browned. Makes 1 9-inch pie.

3	c rhubarb
2	c hulled strawberries
1½	c sugar
½	tsp salt
¼	tsp Stone-Buhr all-purpose flour
3	eggs
2	tbsp Stone-Buhr wheat germ
2	tbsp soft butter or margarine
1	9-inch pie shell and lattice top

DESSERTS

Clockwise from left: Indian Pudding with whipped cream p.140, Carrot Cake with butter cream frosting p.145, Cherry Cream Crunch p.139

DESSERTS

Americans like desserts. Adults and children both savor sweets. The dessert is an added attraction to any meal. It should be chosen carefully. A heavy dessert, such as pie or cake, goes with a light meal. But, if the meal you have planned is a heavy one, the dessert should be something that is light and not too filling.

Desserts love to be garnished. Plain desserts seem more elegant when you use your imagination in serving them. Many recipes for cakes can be baked in a variety of pieces of equipment. For a change, try baking a cake in a tube pan or as cupcakes. However, recipes that call for using a tube pan should be baked in one for best results. A cake recipe that calls for 2 cups of flour will generally make:

- two 8-inch layers 1½ inches deep
- one 9 x 5 x 5 inch loaf cake
- one 13 x 9½ x 2 inch cake
- 1½ dozen large cupcakes
- 2 dozen medium cupcakes

Bake cookies in pans that are bright and shiny. When making cookie bars, they are easier to remove from the pan if the pan is greased and then lined with waxed paper or brown paper. Bar cookies are done when the dough pulls away from the sides of the pan. Another way to know if bar cookies and soft cookies have been baked long enough is to touch the top lightly with the fingers. The top of the cookies should spring back. Crisp cookies are done when they are fairly firm and lightly browned around the edges.

To test the doneness of a cake, touch the top lightly with your finger—the slight indentation will spring back when the cake is done. Loaf and batter bread have a much thicker batter than cakes and they should be tested with a toothpick. When the toothpick, inserted in the center of the pan, comes out clean, the bread is done.

Cookies should be removed from the baking pan right when you take the pan out of the oven. They may be cooled on brown paper or a wire rack. Allow the cookies to cool completely before stacking them on a plate or placing in a cookie jar.

Cakes with shortening in them should be allowed to cool in the pan for 10 minutes and then removed from the pan and placed on a wire rack.

Puddings may be served warm or cold. Indian pudding and the double chocolate whole wheat pudding are delightful when served warm with ice cream or whipped cream.

APPLE COFFEE CAKE

Watch this coffee cake carefully near the end of the baking period. If it starts to get too brown and it is not completely baked, cover the top with foil and continue baking.

Sift together all-purpose flour, rice flour, ½ cup sugar, baking powder, salt, and cinnamon. Add nuts. Stir in apple. Blend together egg, milk and oil. Add to flour mixture and mix well. Turn into a greased 9-inch round cake pan. Spoon sour cream over the top in spiral fashion, leaving center uncovered. Sprinkle remaining ½ cup sugar over top; scatter on 2 tablespoons bran flakes. Bake in a 400 degree oven for about 40 minutes or until done. Let cool slightly before cutting into wedges. Best when served warm. Yields 6 servings.

1½	c sifted Stone-Buhr all-purpose flour
½	c Stone-Buhr rice flour
½	c sugar
2	tsp baking powder
½	tsp salt
½	tsp cinnamon
½	c chopped walnuts
1	large peeled apple, shredded
1	egg
½	c milk
3	tbsp oil
½	c sour cream
½	c sugar
2	tbsp Stone-Buhr bran flakes

APPLESAUCE RAISIN CAKE

This allergy recipe contains no wheat, eggs, or milk. It is not as light as most applesauce cakes but has a good flavor.

Combine oat flour, oats, sugar, salt, soda, and spices. Add shortening, eggs, and vanilla. Beat until smooth, about 2 minutes. Stir in applesauce and raisins. Pour batter into greased 8-inch square baking pan. Bake in preheated 350 degree oven about 60 minutes or until done. Cool; cover pan and store one day before serving. Yields 9 servings.

1¼	c Stone-Buhr oat flour
½	c Stone-Buhr quick oats
⅔	c sugar
1	tsp salt
1	tsp soda
2	tsp cinnamon
½	tsp nutmeg
½	c soft shortening
2	eggs, beaten
1	tsp vanilla
1	c raisins
1	c applesauce

PEACH COBBLER

This recipe can be used with any canned fruit you happen to have. Peaches are pretty because they have such a nice color.

Peach Base:
- ⅓ c sugar
- 2 tbsp Stone-Buhr pancake mix
- 1 No. 2½ can sliced peaches
- 1 tbsp lemon juice
- Butter or margarine

Topping:
- 2 c Stone-Buhr pancake mix
- ¼ c sugar
- 2 eggs, beaten
- 1 c milk
- ⅓ c oil

Combine sugar and pancake mix with 1 cup juice drained from peaches; cook over low heat until thickened. Place peach slices, lemon juice and thickened sauce in 10x6x1½-inch baking pan; dot with butter.

For topping, mix pancake mix and sugar. Add beaten eggs and milk to dry ingredients; stir until fairly smooth. Stir in oil. Drop batter by spoonfuls over fruit. Bake at 425 degrees 25 to 30 minutes. Serve warm with peach syrup or cream, plain or whipped. Makes 9-12 servings.

RHUBARB COBBLER

Stone-Buhr pancake mixes can be used in a variety of ways. The regular pancake mix gives a nice mild flavor. For whole wheat lovers, try using Stone-Buhr whole wheat pancake mix.

Base:
- ¾ c sugar
- ⅓ c Stone-Buhr pancake mix
- 1 tsp grated lemon rind
- 4 c fresh rhubarb cut in ½-inch pieces (about 1½ lbs)

Topping:
- ¾ c Stone-Buhr pancake mix
- ½ c sugar
- 1 egg, beaten
- ¼ c melted butter or margarine

For base, combine sugar, pancake mix and rind. Add rhubarb; toss lightly. Place in buttered 9-inch square baking pan. For topping, combine pancake mix and sugar. Add egg; stir until mixture resembles coarse crumbs. Sprinkle evenly over rhubarb base. Drizzle with melted butter. Bake at 375 degrees for 35 to 40 minutes. Serve warm with ice cream or half and half. Makes 6 servings.

RHUBARB SQUARES

This rhubarb recipe tastes delicious with fresh or frozen rhubarb—be sure to cut down the amount of sugar in the recipe if the frozen rhubarb you are using has been sweetened.

Mix first 5 ingredients till crumbly; press ⅔'s of the mixture into a 11½ x 7-inch pan or 9-inch square pan. Cover with rhubarb. Combine remaining ingredients, bring to boiling point and boil 1 minute. Pour over the rhubarb and sprinkle with remaining crumb mixture. Bake at 350 degrees for 1 hour or until done. Serve warm or cold, topped with ice cream, if desired. Makes 9 squares.

1	c sifted Stone-Buhr all-purpose flour
¾	c Stone-Buhr wheat flakes
1	tsp cinnamon
1	c brown sugar
½	c melted butter or margarine
4	c cut up rhubarb (about 1½ lbs).
1	c sugar
1	c water
3	tbsp cornstarch

APPLESAUCE CAKE

Applesauce cake is good with caramel or spice frosting.

Cream butter and sugar. Add egg and mix well. Stir in applesauce, raisins and nuts. Sift dry ingredients together; add to applesauce mixture and blend well. Pour into greased 9-inch layer pan and bake at 375 degrees for 30 to 40 minutes or until done. Serves 6-8.

½	c butter or margarine
1	c sugar
1	egg
1	c applesauce (unsweetened)
1	c chopped raisins
¼	c chopped nuts
1½	c Stone-Buhr all-purpose flour
½	c Stone-Buhr rice flour
1	tsp soda
1	tsp cinnamon
1	tsp allspice
½	tsp salt
½	tsp baking powder
½	tsp cloves

ⓐ RICE FLOUR CAKE

⅓   c shortening
½   c sugar
2   eggs
⅔   c Stone-Buhr rice flour
⅓   c Stone-Buhr potato starch
1   tbsp baking powder
½   tsp salt
1   pkg of Dream Whip (optional)
⅔   c milk
1   tsp vanilla

This is the most delightful recipe for a wheat free cake that you will ever find. It was developed by a Home Economics student doing an individual project in food and nutrition.

Cream together the shortening and sugar. Add eggs and beat well. Sift together the rice flour, potato starch, baking powder, salt and Dream Whip. The powdered topping may be eliminated, but it helps give the cake a nicer volume. Add the dry ingredients alternately with the milk and vanilla to the creamed mixture. Pour into a greased 8-inch cake pan and bake at 350 degrees for 25-30 minutes or until done. Cool for 10-15 minutes before removing the cake from pan. Makes 1 8-inch cake.

ⓐ COCOA CAKE

1¼   c sifted Stone-Buhr all-purpose flour
½   tsp baking soda
¼   tsp salt
1   c sugar
¼   c cocoa
¼   c vegetable shortening
¾   c water

This cake is one you can make when people want to cut down on saturated fats. It is easy to make up ahead without the water and store just like a cake mix until you're ready to use it.

Sift together the flour, baking soda, salt and sugar. Add cocoa and mix well with a spoon. Cut the shortening into the dry ingredients. This dry mix can then be stored for several weeks or until you want to use it. When ready to use, add water and stir just until mixed. Pour into a greased 8-inch round cake pan and bake at 350 degrees for 45 minutes or until done. Makes 1 8-inch layer.

APRICOT CAKE

This sugary cake has a delicious brandy flavor. I like to serve it while it is still warm.

Cream butter and sugar until light, add eggs one at a time and beat well. Sift pastry flour and baking powder together; stir into creamed mixture. Spread in greased 8-inch square pan. Arrange apricots in batter, cut side up. Place brandy in apricots on cake. Bake at 375 degrees for about 35 minutes. Top with whipped cream if desired. Serves 6.

½	c butter
½	c sugar
2	eggs
1	c sifted Stone-Buhr pastry flour
1	tsp baking powder
12	canned apricot halves, drained
3	tbsp brandy
1	tbsp butter or margarine
1	tsp grated orange rind
½	c sugar for topping
½	c whipped cream

SOFT GINGERBREAD

If you really like a strong ginger flavor, increase the amount of ginger to 1½ teaspoons. You can use 100% stone ground whole wheat flour instead of the fine whole wheat flour. The gingerbread will be a little coarser in texture.

Mix dry ingredients together. Combine oil, eggs, milk and molasses. Pour into dry ingredients and beat to mix well. Bake in a greased and floured 9 x 13-inch pan for 35 to 45 minutes at 350 degrees or until firm to the touch. Cut into squares. Serves 12.

3	c Stone-Buhr whole wheat pastry flour
1	tsp ginger
1	tbsp cinnamon
1	tsp cloves
½	tsp salt
1	tsp soda
1	c sugar
1	c oil
3	eggs
1	c sour milk
1	c molasses

PICNIC CAKE

1	c Stone-Buhr quick cooking oatmeal
1¼	c boiling water
½	c shortening
1	c sugar, white
1	c brown sugar
1	tsp vanilla
2	eggs
1⅓	c sifted Stone-Buhr all-purpose flour
1	tsp cinnamon
1	tsp nutmeg
½	tsp salt
1	tsp soda

Broiled Topping:
⅓	c butter or margarine
⅔	c brown sugar
1	c flaked coconut
½	c chopped nuts
½	c Stone-Buhr wheat flakes
¼	c evaporated milk or cream
1	tsp vanilla

This cake is moist and keeps well. The broiled topping is very good and can be used on any of your favorite cakes.

Gradually stir oatmeal into boiling water; let stand 20 minutes. Cream shortening; gradually add white and brown sugar. Add vanilla and eggs. Sift together dry ingredients and add alternately with oatmeal, beating well after each addition. Bake in greased 9x13x2-inch pan at 350 degrees for 35 minutes, or until done.

For broiled topping, combine ingredients thoroughly. Spread on hot cake and place under broiler until slightly brown. Serves 12 to 15.

APPLE STRUDEL

This is one of the best apple strudels in the world. Once you try this, you'll make it whenever you need a special dessert.

Make a well in 1½ cups flour. Drop in lard, egg and ¼ cup lukewarm water; mix with hands. Add about 2 tablespoons water to make a soft dough. Toss dough down hard on lightly floured board 10 to 15 minutes until it "thuds" and is smooth. Form ball. Cover with inverted bowl and let stand ½ hour. Remove jewelry as it may tear dough. Spread tablecloth on card table; dust with flour, Roll dough to a 12-inch square. Put hands under dough, palms down. Slowly, stretch dough until about 36 x 36", the dough will be as thin as tissue paper. Cut off 2-inches of thick outer edges. Brush with ¼ cup melted butter. Combine thoroughly all filling ingredients. Sprinkle evenly over ⅔'s of the dough, leaving a 2-inch margin on 3 sides. Fold side edges over about 2 inches. Starting at the end that has the filling, lift cloth and gently roll up the strudel. Place on greased pan. Quickly brush with melted butter. Bake at 400 degrees 40 minutes. Serves 12.

1½	c unsifted Stone-Buhr all-purpose flour
1	tbsp soft lard or shortening
1	egg, beaten
¼	c lukewarm water + 2 tbsp
¼	c melted butter or margarine

Filling:

4	c finely chopped, pared, tart apples
¾	c fine dry bread crumbs
¼	c brown sugar
¼	c granulated sugar
2	tsp cinnamon
½	c raisins
½	c finely chopped walnuts
2	tbsp melted butter or margarine

CHERRY CREAM CRUNCH

½ c butter or margarine
½ c brown sugar, firmly packed
1 tsp vanilla
1 c sifted Stone-Buhr all-purpose flour
½ tsp salt
½ tsp cinnamon
1 c flaked or chopped shredded
   coconut
½ c Stone-Buhr wheat flakes
½ c chopped walnuts
Filling:
2 eggs, slightly beaten
1 can (15 oz) sweetened condensed
   milk
1 tbsp grated lemon rind
¼ c fresh lemon juice
¼ tsp salt
1 can (1 lb 4 oz) cherry pie filling

Any of the Stone-Buhr flake products are good in this recipe. Barley flakes and quick oats give a soft crumb; rice flakes will be crisper.

Cream butter in a large mixing bowl; gradually add brown sugar and vanilla. Mix well. Sift flour, salt and cinnamon; add to butter mixture. Stir in coconut, wheat flakes and walnuts. Press 2½ cups of crumb mixture into bottom of ungreased 9x13-inch baking dish. Bake at 375 degrees for 12 minutes. Prepare the lemon filling by combining the slightly beaten eggs, sweetened condensed milk, grated lemon rind, fresh lemon juice and salt. Stir until mixture thickens. Remove crust from the oven and spread with lemon filling. Sprinkle with remaining crumb mixture. Return to oven and bake at 375 degrees 15 to 18 minutes, until delicately browned. Chill before serving plain or with whipped cream. Serves 9 to 12.

BREAD PUDDING

6 slices Oroweat raisin bread
4 c milk, scalded
1 tbsp butter or margarine
¼ tsp salt
¾ c sugar
4 slightly beaten eggs
1 tsp vanilla

Bread pudding is an old fashioned dessert that is fun to make during the winter. It is a nice way to use up bread that is starting to stale.

Soak bread in milk for 5 minutes. Add butter, salt and sugar. Pour slowly over eggs. Add vanilla and mix well. Pour into greased baking dish. Bake at 350 degrees in pan of hot water about 50 minutes or until firm. Makes 8 servings.

VANILLA PUDDING ⓐ

Puddings made with rice flour are not as stiff as those made with cornstarch. They have more of a custard-like consistency. Try pouring hot pudding over pieces of slightly stale cake and then top each serving with whipped cream.

Mix together sugar, rice flour and salt; gradually blend in milk. Cook over medium heat, stirring constantly until mixture thickens. Cook 2 or 3 minutes more. Add vanilla. Pour into 5 or 6 sherbets or individual molds rinsed with cold water. Cover with plastic wrap. Chill until firm. Unmold. Serve topped with chilled fruit cocktail. Makes 4 to 5 servings.

⅓	c sugar
6	tbsp Stone-Buhr rice flour
¼	tsp salt
2½	c milk
1½	tsp vanilla

BAKED INDIAN PUDDING

Although this recipe takes many hours before it is ready to eat, it takes very little of the cook's time. The long slow cooking results in a delicious caramelized flavor. Prepare this on a cold stormy day. Its fragrance will warm your kitchen.

Scald 3 cups of milk; pour over cornmeal. Add remaining ingredients. Mix thoroughly. Pour into buttered 1½ quart casserole. Place in 250 degree oven. After pudding has been in oven for 20 minutes, pour in remaining cup of cold milk and stir carefully. Continue baking for 5 hours. To insure proper consistency, stir carefully 4 or 5 times during first 1½ hours of baking. Serve warm with whipped cream or ice cream. Makes 4 to 5 servings.

1	qt milk
½	c Stone-Buhr yellow cornmeal
½	c sugar
¼	c molasses
1	tsp salt
2	tbsp butter or margarine

CHOCOLATE PUDDING

Follow directions for Vanilla Pudding, but increase sugar to ½ cup and mix ⅓ cup cocoa with sugar, rice flour and salt. (Or use 2, 1-ounce squares unsweetened chocolate, cut up, added with the milk, instead of cocoa).

DOUBLE CHOCOLATE PUDDING

½ c sugar
1 c unsifted Stone-Buhr whole wheat pastry flour
2 tsp baking powder
2 tbsp cocoa
¼ tsp salt
2 tbsp butter or margarine, melted
½ c milk
1 tsp vanilla
2 tbsp cocoa
½ c sugar
1 c water

This is really a new twist to pudding making. This recipe has a very rich chocolaty flavor. It can be eaten warm with a little cream or just plain.

Mix together ½ cup sugar, flour, baking powder, 2 tablespoons cocoa and salt. Stir in a mixture of melted butter, milk and vanilla. Mix thoroughly and pour into a 2-quart baking dish. Mix together 2 tablespoons cocoa and ½ cup sugar; sprinkle over batter in baking dish. Carefully pour water over the top of all. Bake at 350 degrees about 45 minutes or until crusty on top. Cool and serve topped with ice cream or whipped cream. Makes 4 to 6 servings.

RICE PUDDING

4 c water
¾ c long grain brown rice
¾ c sugar
¼ c white raisins
5 tbsp butter or margarine
3″ piece vanilla bean
3″ cinnamon stick
3 c milk
½ c chopped apricots
3 eggs, separated
¼ tsp cream of tartar

This rice pudding has a delightfully tart taste from the dried fruits. Although it takes awhile to prepare, it is one of the most delicious rice puddings you can make.

Bring 4 cups water to a boil. Add rice and boil for 20 minutes. Drain rice in a sieve. Place rice, sugar, raisins, 3 tablespoons butter, vanilla beans, cinnamon stick and milk in a saucepan. Bring to a boil, cover and cook over low heat, stirring occasionally for about 1¼ hours, or until most of the milk is absorbed. Stir in remaining 2 tablespoons butter. Spread out in a pan and let it cool. Remove the vanilla and cinnamon pieces from the rice and mix in ½ c chopped apricots and 3 egg yolks. In a bowl, beat the 3 egg whites and cream of tartar until soft peaks form. Fold gently into rice mixture. Pour into a mold and place in a pan of hot water. Bake at 325 degrees for 1 hour. Remove from oven and let stand at room temperature for 2 hours before serving.

POTATO SPONGE CAKE @

This sponge cake is light and airy and stays moist for several days. It is an excellent cake to make for those on a wheat-free diet.

Separate 6 of the 7 eggs. Beat the 6 egg yolks and one whole egg until thick. Gradually add 1 cup of sugar. Add the lemon juice and lemon rind and beat well. Gradually add potato starch and beat until well blended. Add the cream of tartar and salt to the egg whites. Beat until very foamy. Slowly add remaining ½ cup sugar, beating until egg whites form stiff peaks. Fold gently but thoroughly into egg yolk mixture. Place in an ungreased 10″ tube pan. Bake in a 350 degree oven about 55 minutes or until cake springs back when touched gently with the fingers. Invert pan and cool thoroughly before removing from the pan.

7	eggs
1½	c sugar
1	tbsp and 2 tsp lemon juice
2	tsp grated lemon rind
¾	c sifted Stone-Buhr potato starch
¼	tsp cream of tartar
	Dash of salt

CHOCOLATE YEAST CAKE

This is an old fashioned kind of chocolate cake, leavened with yeast. Test for doneness of this cake by inserting a toothpick in the center. The toothpick will come out clean when the cake is done.

Sift flour with soda and salt. Cream shortening and sugar until fluffy. Add eggs one at a time, beating after each one. Soften yeast in ¼ cup lukewarm water, add to creamed mixture and beat well. Add milk, chocolate and vanilla. Add dry ingredients and beat for 5 minutes. Pour batter into greased and floured tube pan and allow to stand, covered for 1 hour. Bake in 350 degree oven for about 1 hour and 25 minutes or until done. Cool 5 minutes in pan, then turn out. When cool, dust with powdered sugar. Serves 10-12.

3	c sifted Stone-Buhr all-purpose flour
1	tsp soda
½	tsp salt
1	c butter (or margarine or shortening)
2	c sugar
3	eggs
1	cake or pkg. active dry yeast
¼	c lukewarm water
1	c milk
2	squares of chocolate melted or 6 tbsp cocoa
1	tsp vanilla
	Powdered sugar

LINZERTORTE

1½	c sifted Stone-Buhr all-purpose flour
⅛	tsp ground cloves
¼	tsp cinnamon
1	c finely ground unblanched almonds
½	c sugar
1	tsp grated lemon peel
2	hard-cooked egg yolks, mashed
1	c unsalted butter, softened
2	egg yolks
1	tsp vanilla
1½	c thick raspberry jam
1	egg, lightly beaten
2	tbsp light cream
	confectioners' sugar

A very famous torte that is easy to prepare. Unsalted butter is used because it gives a delicate flavor.

Sift the flour, cloves, and cinnamon together into a deep mixing bowl. Add almonds, sugar, lemon peel, and mashed cooked egg yolks. Beat in the butter, egg yolks and vanilla until the mixture is smooth. Form the dough into a ball, wrap in wax paper and refrigerate for 1 hour, or until firm. Take out ¾ of the dough.

Lightly grease a round 9-by-1-inch false-bottomed cake pan. Add the dough, and with your fingers, press and push it out so that it covers the bottom and sides of the pan, making a shell ¼-inch thick. Spoon in raspberry jam and spread it evenly. Roll out the rest of the dough into a 6-by-9 inch rectangle ¼-inch thick.

Cut the dough into 6 strips about ½-inch wide. Lay one of the strips across the center of the jam and add a strip on each side. Rotate the pan about ¼ of the way to your left and repeat the pattern with the other strips so that they create Xs with the first 3.

Run a sharp knife around the top of the pan to loosen the part of the bottom dough that extends above the strips. Press this down with your fingers into a border about ¼-inch thick. Lightly beat the whole egg with the cream, and brush it on the pastry. Refrigerate for ½ hour. Preheat oven to 350 degrees.

Bake the torte for 45-50 minutes, or until it is lightly browned. Let the torte cool for 5 minutes and remove from pan. Sprinkle it with confectioner's sugar. Serves 8.

STRAWBERRY CREME CREPES

This is one of my very favorite recipes. Try serving it for a brunch or as a dessert. Making crepes is easy if you use a well seasoned skillet or one that is teflon lined. I make all the crepes first, stacking them and covering them with a towel until they are all prepared. Then I fill them all at once and they are ready to serve.

Combine pancake mix, eggs, milk and lemon peel; mix well. Set aside. Hull and slice strawberries. Place 1 cup strawberries in a bowl and sprinkle with ½ cup sugar. For filling, combine cream cheese, powdered sugar, vanilla and remaining 1 cup strawberries and blend until smooth.

Melt a small amount of butter in a 6-inch skillet. Pour 2 tablespoons of batter into pan and rotate quickly so batter covers the bottom. Cook over medium heat 1 to 2 minutes on each side (see illus. p. 69). Spread about 1 tablespoon strawberry filling on each crepe. Roll up and serve with sweetened strawberries. Serves 5 to 6.

1	c Stone-Buhr pancake mix
6	eggs
1	c milk
1	tsp grated lemon peel
2	c fresh strawberries
½	c sugar
8	oz cream cheese
½	c powdered sugar
¼	tsp vanilla
	Butter

CHOCOLATE CAKE

A nice chocolate cake for those who are allergic to wheat. I like the coffee flavor and loose texture of this cake.

Stir and measure rye flour. Mix with baking powder and salt. Stir hot coffee or hot water gradually into cocoa; when smooth, let cool. Cream shortening and sugar until light and fluffy. Add cooled cocoa mixture and beat thoroughly. Add dry ingredients alternately with milk, beating well after each addition. Beat egg whites to the stiff peak stage; fold into batter. Spread batter in two 8-inch layer pans which have been greased. Bake at 375 degrees 25 to 30 minutes or until done. Serves 8-10.

2	c unsifted Stone-Buhr rye flour
2	tsp baking powder
½	tsp salt
½	c cocoa
½	c hot strong coffee or hot water
½	c shortening
1½	c sugar
1	tsp vanilla
3	egg yolks
½	c milk
3	egg whites

BLACK BOTTOM CUPCAKES

8 oz cream cheese, softened
1 egg
⅓ c sugar
⅛ tsp salt
1 6-oz pkg chocolate chips
1½ c sifted Stone-Buhr all-purpose flour
1 c sugar
1 tsp soda
¼ c cocoa
½ tsp salt
1 c water
⅓ c oil
1 tbsp vinegar
1 tsp vanilla

For chocolate lovers! These delicious cupcakes have a creamy center. Pack them in lunches.

Place cream cheese, egg, sugar and salt in a bowl. Beat well and stir in chocolate chips. Set aside. Beat all remaining ingredients until blended. Fill cupcake liners ⅓ full. Top each with a heaping teaspoon of cream cheese mixture. Bake at 350 degrees for 25 to 30 minutes. Makes about 18 cupcakes.

⊙ CARROT SPICE CAKE

1½ c grated carrots
1⅓ c sugar
1⅓ c water
1 c raisins
¼ c butter or margarine
1 tsp cinnamon
1 tsp cloves
1 tsp nutmeg
2 c Stone-Buhr sifted all-purpose flour
1 tsp baking powder
½ tsp soda
¼ tsp salt
½ c chopped nuts

This carrot cake is my favorite. It is moist, spicy and keeps well. Frost it with a fluffy boiled or butter cream frosting.

Place carrots, sugar, water, raisins, butter and spices in a pan. Bring to a boil and simmer for 5 minutes. Cool. Meanwhile, sift flour, baking powder, soda and salt together. Add the dry ingredients and nuts to the carrot mixture. Stir until blended. Pour into a well greased and floured 9-inch ring mold. Bake at 375 degrees for about 50 minutes or until done. Makes 1 ring. Frost with white glaze frosting if desired.

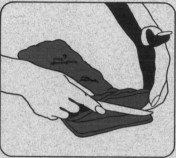

PASTRY STRIP SHORTCAKES

Shortcakes like these are sure to be a favorite. Try serving it as a dessert or as the main attraction with coffee.

Place 1 cup of the flour in a bowl and cut in ½ cup of the butter until fine. Mix in 2 tablespoons cold water, pat into a ball; roll on a floured board into an even 8x12-inch rectangle. Cut into 2 strips, each 4x12-inches. Place on baking sheet. Combine 1 cup water and ½ cup butter in a saucepan and bring to a boil. Remove from heat, add the remaining 1 cup flour and beat hard. Add eggs one at a time, beating well after each addition. Mix in extract. Spread paste evenly over both pastry strips. Bake at 400 degrees for 45 minutes or until browned. Blend sugar and cream; frost pastry tops; sprinkle with nuts. These may be filled with strawberries and whipped cream if desired. Makes 2 strips, each serving 6.

2	c unsifted Stone-Buhr all-purpose flour
1	c (½ lb) butter or margarine
	Water
4	eggs
¼	tsp almond extract
1	c powdered sugar (unsifted)
2	tbsp light cream
⅓	c sliced or slivered almonds, toasted

ⓐ DOUBLE CHOCOLATE BROWNIES

2 eggs
1 c sugar
2 squares unsweetened chocolate, melted
⅓ c butter or margarine, melted
1 tsp vanilla
⅔ c rice flour
½ tsp baking powder
¼ tsp salt
½ c semi sweet chocolate pieces (chips)
¾ c miniature marshmallows

This allergy recipe is just delicious. The brownies are very moist and it is best to let them stand for a few hours before slicing.

Beat eggs until light; gradually beat in sugar. Stir in melted chocolate, butter and vanilla. Sift rice flour with baking powder and salt; add to chocolate mixture. Stir until blended. Stir in chocolate pieces and marshmallows. Spread in a greased 8x8 inch pan. Bake at 350 degrees for 35 minutes or until done. Cool and cut into bars. Makes 18 brownies.

SESAME TOFFEE BARS

¼ c Stone-Buhr sesame seeds
1 c butter or margarine
1 c packed brown sugar
1 egg, beaten
1 tsp vanilla
2 c slfted Stone-Buhr all-purpose flour
¼ tsp cinnamon
¼ tsp allspice
⅛ tsp nutmeg
½ c chopped nuts
12 oz semi-sweet chocolate pieces

Cut these cookies into small squares the next time you have open house or a party. They are very pretty by themselves or on a tray with a variety of other sweets.

Toast sesame seeds in 350 degree oven for 15 minutes, or until golden brown. Cream butter and sugar. Add egg and vanilla; mix well. Sift flour with spices. Add to creamed mixture and blend. Stir in nuts. Spread ¼-inch thick in 13 x 15-inch rectangle on a greased baking sheet. Bake at 350 degrees for 20 minutes. While baking, melt chocolate pieces over boiling water. Spread chocolate over cookies while still hot. Sprinkle top with sesame seeds and cut into bars while warm. Makes approximately 4 dozen cookies.

SCOTCH TOFFEE

Remember to score this toffee into squares while it is still warm so that it will cut into even pieces. This is a very brittle, but tasty confection.

Pour butter over oats and rice flakes; mix well. Add sugar, syrup, salt and vanilla; mix well. Grease a 7 x 11-inch metal baking pan. Line with foil and allow foil to stick out over edges of pan. Grease foil well. Pack mixture into foil lined pan, score. Bake at 450 degrees for 12 to 15 minutes. Cool. Loosen edges of foil; invert pan, tap firmly against bread board so that mixture falls out of the pan. Peel off foil. Spread melted chocolate over bar and sprinkle with nuts. Chill; cut into squares. Store in refrigerator. Makes 3 dozen.

⅓ c butter or margarine, melted
1 c Stone-Buhr quick oats
1 c Stone-Buhr rice flakes
½ c firmly packed brown sugar
¼ c dark corn syrup
½ tsp salt
1 tsp vanilla
Topping:
1 6-oz pkg (1 c) melted chocolate chips
¼ c chopped nuts

SOY BANANA BARS

This recipe is a nice variation of a banana bar. The nuts, spices, and soy combine well with the bananas. These bars will stay moist for several days.

Stir all dry ingredients together, including dry milk powder. Add brown sugar and nuts and mix well. Make a well and add oil, eggs, milk and mashed bananas. Stir just until moistened. Bake in ungreased 9 x 13-inch pan at 350 degrees for about 45 minutes or until cake shrinks slightly from sides of the pan. Cut into bars. Makes 24 bars.

1 c Stone-Buhr whole wheat flour
1 c Stone-Buhr soy flour
1 tbsp baking powder
1 c dry milk powder
½ tsp salt
1 tsp cinnamon
½ tsp allspice
½ tsp nutmeg
1 c walnuts
1 c brown sugar
2 eggs, beaten
½ c oil
½ c milk
1½ c mashed bananas

CHOCOLATE-OATMEAL CRUNCHIES

1½	c sifted Stone-Buhr all-purpose flour
1	tsp salt
¾	tsp soda
¾	c shortening
¾	c granulated sugar
¾	c packed brown sugar
2	eggs
1	tsp vanilla
1	c Stone-Buhr cereal mates
1	pkg (6 oz) semi-sweet chocolate pieces
1	pkg (4 oz) shredded coconut

These are a nice variation of oatmeal cookies. Coconut can be omitted if you prefer.

Sift flour, salt, and soda together. Cream shortening and sugars until light. Add eggs and vanilla and beat well. Stir in sifted dry ingredients. Add remaining ingredients and mix well. Drop teaspoonfuls 2-inches apart on ungreased cookie sheets. Bake at 350 degrees for 15 minutes. Remove from sheets and cool on cake racks. Makes about 4 dozen.

PEANUT BUTTER COOKIES

1	c sifted Stone-Buhr all-purpose flour
½	tsp soda
½	tsp salt
½	c shortening
¾	c firmly packed brown sugar
1	egg
1	tsp vanilla
½	c peanut butter
½	c Stone-Buhr oatmeal
½	c Stone-Buhr rice flakes

These cookies are an interesting variation of peanut butter cookies because they have a crunchy texture.

Sift together flour, soda and salt. Cream shortening and sugar. Blend in egg, vanilla, and peanut butter. Beat until smooth. Add dry ingredients and mix well. Stir in oats and rice flakes. Drop onto greased cookie sheets. Bake at 350 degrees for 12 to 15 minutes or until lightly browned. Makes 3 dozen cookies.

COCONUT PEANUT BUTTER BARS

These are really delicious. The people in the Mill kitchen always eat more than one. Take these to your next bake sale—everyone will want the recipe.

Sift flour, baking powder and salt together. Cream margarine, peanut butter and sugar. Stir in eggs and vanilla; mix well. Add flour mixture and coconut. Spread evenly in greased 7 x 11 x 1½-inch cake pan. Bake at 350 degrees for 25 to 30 minutes, or until top springs back when lightly touched—or bake in greased 8 x 8-inch square pan at 350 degrees for 30 to 35 minutes. Cut into bars and roll in confectioners sugar while warm, if desired. Makes about 16 bars.

1	c sifted Stone-Buhr flour
1	tsp baking powder
¼	tsp salt
⅓	c butter or margarine
½	c peanut butter
1	c sugar
2	eggs, beaten
1	tsp vanilla
1	c flaked coconut

ONE-A-DAY BANANA BARS

These are called one-a-day banana bars because they are so nutritious. You may omit the chocolate chips if you want to.

Cream together margarine, sugar, and brown sugar until light and fluffy. Add egg and vanilla; beat well. Stir in mashed bananas. Stir together flour, rye flour, baking powder and salt. Add to banana mixture and beat until combined. Stir in chocolate pieces. Spread evenly in a greased 15½ x 10½-inch baking pan. Bake at 350 degrees for 25 minutes or until done. Cool and cut in squares. May substitute butterscotch chips, if desired. Makes 24 bars.

¾	c butter or margarine
⅔	c sugar
⅔	c brown sugar
1	egg
1	tsp vanilla
2	medium sized ripe bananas, mashed
1½	c sifted Stone-Buhr all-purpose flour
½	c Stone-Buhr rye or whole wheat flour
2	tsp baking powder
½	tsp salt
1	6-oz pkg chocolate pieces

QUICK DATE BARS

1 c Stone-Buhr pancake mix
½ c brown sugar
1 egg
¼ c shortening
1 tsp vanilla
¼ c milk
⅓ c chopped dates
⅓ c chopped nuts

What could be quicker than starting date bars with pancake mix? You might try varying this recipe with dried apricots, if you prefer.

Place pancake mix, sugar, egg, shortening, vanilla and milk in a medium-sized bowl. Beat until smooth, about 2 minutes. Stir in chopped dates and nuts. Bake in a greased 7 x 11-inch pan at 350 degrees for 20 to 25 minutes. Cut while warm into squares. Serve plain or rolled in confectioners sugar. Makes 1½ dozen bars.

DREAM BARS

⅓ c butter or margarine
¼ c brown sugar
½ c Stone-Buhr all-purpose flour
1 egg
½ c brown sugar
½ tsp vanilla
1 tbsp Stone-Buhr all-purpose flour
1 tbsp baking powder
½ tsp salt
¾ c coconut
½ c chopped nuts
Powdered sugar

These dream bars are good with ice cream on top. Most people like vanilla with them, but I think coffee is super.

Mix butter, ¼ cup brown sugar and ½ cup flour together until crumbly; press into 8-inch square pan, covering bottom. Bake at 350 degrees for 25 minutes. Set aside. Beat egg and ½ cup brown sugar together and add the vanilla. Mix 1 tablespoon flour, baking powder and salt and add to coconut and nuts. Then add this mixture to egg mixture. Pour into baked crust. Spread evenly. Bake at 350 degrees for 30 minutes. Cool and cut into bars. Sprinkle with powdered sugar. Makes 9 dessert servings or 12 bar cookies.

ALMOND PILLOWS

These are a very special cookie. The flavor is distinct and yet mild and they will melt in your mouth. Be careful not to bake too long or they will become too dry. They are done when just a faint brown.

Cream butter brown sugar and granulated sugar until blended. Add the egg and vanilla and beat until combined. In another bowl stir together the all-purpose flour, pastry flour, baking powder, salt, cardamom, and cinnamon; stir into creamed mixture until blended. Turn mixture out onto a lightly floured board; divide into 4 equal parts. Roll out each to a 15-inch rope; cut rope into 1-inch pieces. Lightly press an almond in the middle of each piece; place on ungreased cookie sheets. Bake in a 350 degree oven for about 15 minutes or until resistant to touch; cool on racks. Makes 60 cookies.

½	c (¼ lb) butter or margarine, softened
½	c firmly packed brown sugar
½	c granulated sugar
1	egg
1	tsp vanilla
1	c Stone-Buhr pastry flour
1	c Stone-Buhr all-purpose flour
1	tsp baking powder
½	tsp salt
¾	tsp ground cardamom
½	tsp ground cinnamon
60	whole blanched almonds

SUNFLOWER SEED COOKIES

These cookies have a good sunflower seed taste. They travel well and you can keep the dough for a few days in the refrigerator if you wish before baking them.

Thoroughly cream together butter, brown sugar and granulated sugar. Add eggs, add vanilla and beat to blend well. Add flour, salt, soda and rolled oats. Mix thoroughly. Gently blend in sunflower seeds. Form in long rolls about 1½-inches in diameter. Wrap in clear plastic film and chill thoroughly. Slice ¼-inch thick. Arrange on ungreased cookie sheet and bake in 350 degree oven for 10 minutes or until lightly browned. Cool on wire racks and store in air-tight containers. Makes about 9 dozen cookies.

1	c butter or margarine
1	c firmly packed brown sugar
1	c granulated sugar
2	eggs
1	tsp vanilla
1½	c unsifted Stone-Buhr all-purpose flour
¾	tsp salt
1	tsp soda
3	c Stone-Buhr quick cooking rolled oats
1	c Stone-Buhr sunflower seeds

OATMEAL COOKIES

```
1    c butter or margarine
1    c sugar
1    c brown sugar
2    eggs
2½   c sifted Stone-Buhr all-purpose flour
1    tsp soda
¾    tsp salt
2    c quick cooking Stone-Buhr
     rolled oats
8    small plain chocolate bars
```

This is a delicious oatmeal cookie. If you'd like, try pressing a walnut half in the center of each chocolate square.

Cream butter and sugars until light and fluffy; add eggs and beat thoroughly. Sift flour with soda and salt. Stir into butter mixture, add rolled oats. Drop from a teaspoon about 2-inches apart on greased cookie sheets. Bake at 375 degrees for 10 to 12 minutes, or until delicately browned. Press 1 small square of chocolate on each cookie before removing from cookie sheet. Makes about 6 dozen cookies.

PINEAPPLE UPSIDE DOWN CAKE

```
Topping:
½    c butter or margarine
1    c brown sugar
⅓    c Stone-Buhr bran flakes
1    can (1 lb, 13½ oz) crushed
     pineapple, well drained
12   maraschino cherries
Batter:
½    c butter or margarine
1    c sugar
2    eggs
2    c sifted Stone-Buhr pastry flour
2½   tsp baking powder
¼    tsp salt
¼    c milk
1    tsp vanilla
```

Upside down cakes are always popular. I like them with lots of topping and not too much cake.

Melt ½ cup butter in a saucepan; stir in brown sugar until it dissolves and add bran flakes. Pour mixture into greased 9 x 13-inch pan. Top with crushed pineapple. Arrange cherries in 3 rows of 4, so that a cherry will be centered in each serving piece.

To prepare batter: Cream butter until light and fluffy, gradually adding sugar. Add eggs 1 at a time, blending well after each addition. Sift dry ingredients, then add them alternately with milk and vanilla to creamed mixture. Pour batter over pineapple and cherries. Bake at 375 degrees for 40 minutes, or until cake tests done. Makes 12 servings.

SUNFLOWER BARS

These sunflower bars are a nice change in bar cookies. The basic dough is rather like a sponge cake and therefore is very light and tasty. You may try coloring the sunflower seeds with food coloring, if you'd like.

In large mixer bowl, beat the three egg yolks; add the granulated sugar and the vanilla, beating till thick and lemon-colored. Sift together flour and baking powder; stir into yolk mixture. Add boiling water; mix well. Fold in stiff-beaten egg white and ½ cup sunflower seeds. Spread evenly in greased 15½ x 10½ x 1-inch baking pan. Bake in 350 degree oven for 20 minutes or till done. Cool.

Frost with Butter Icing: In small mixer bowl, combine the one egg yolk, the melted butter or margarine, and confectioners' sugar. Beat till smooth. Add enough milk to make of spreading consistency, about 1 tablespoon. Spread over cooled sunflower bars. Sprinkle chopped sunflower seeds over the top, pressing lightly into frosting. Makes 36 bars.

Batter:
3	egg yolks
1	c granulated sugar
1	tsp vanilla
1	c sifted Stone-Buhr all-purpose flour
1	tsp baking powder
½	c boiling water
4	stiffly-beaten egg whites
½	c Stone-Buhr sunflower seeds

Frosting:
1	egg yolk
6	tbsp butter or margarine, melted
2	c sifted confectioners sugar
1	tbsp milk
1	c finely chopped Stone-Buhr sunflower seeds

PEANUT BUTTER CHEWS

This allergy recipe does not use wheat flour. These cookies are chewy and remind me of old fashioned peanut butter cookies.

Cream shortening, peanut butter and add the sugar. Mix in egg and then all the remaining ingredients. Drop by spoonfuls on greased baking sheet. Flatten slightly with a fork. Bake at 325 degrees for about 12 minutes, or until brown. Makes 3 dozen.

½	c shortening
½	c peanut butter (if desired)
1	c brown sugar
1	egg
1	c Stone-Buhr quick oats
1	c Stone-Buhr rye flour
1	tbsp baking powder
½	tsp cinnamon
½	tsp salt
¼	c water
½	c chopped raisins

VINEYARD RAISIN DROPS

½ c burgundy wine
1 c raisins
1 c butter or margarine
1½ c packed brown sugar
3 eggs
½ tsp vanilla
1 tbsp grated lemon peel
½ c Stone-Buhr wheat flakes
2½ c unsifted Stone-Buhr all-purpose flour
1 tsp cinnamon
¼ tsp cloves
¼ tsp allspice
1 tsp soda
½ tsp salt
1 c chopped walnuts or pecans

Wine in cookies—what a delightful way to enhance the flavor of the raisins in these cookies! I especially like them frosted with a buttercream frosting.

Bring wine to a boil. Remove from heat and add raisins. Let stand. Cream margarine and sugar. Beat in eggs, one at a time. Add vanilla, lemon peel and wheat flakes. Sift flour with spices, soda and salt. Add to creamed mixture alternately with raisin-wine mixture. Stir in nuts, mixing lightly. Drop by teaspoonfuls on greased cookie sheet. Bake at 375 degrees about 12 minutes or until done. Makes about 6 dozen. Add frosting, if desired.

BUTTERSCOTCH CHIP COOKIES

1 c butter or margarine
1 c brown sugar
2 eggs
1 tsp vanilla
2 c Stone-Buhr soy flour
¼ c Stone-Buhr rice flour
1 tsp soda
½ tsp salt
2 6-oz pkg butterscotch chips

The butterscotch chip flavor combines so nicely with the soy flour. This is one of the best cookies that can be made without wheat flour. These keep well. Substitute chocolate chips in the recipe if you wish.

Cream margarine and brown sugar together. Beat in eggs and add vanilla. Mix dry ingredients together and add to creamed mixture. Blend in butterscotch chips. Drop onto greased cookie sheet. Bake at 350 degrees about 10 to 12 minutes. Chocolate chips may be used instead of butterscotch chips.

GRAIN NUTRIENTS
nutrients in the edible portion of 1 pound of food as purchased

	food energy calories	protein	fat	carbohydrates	calcium	phosphorus	iron	sodium	potassium	vitamin A units	thiamine	riboflavin	niacin
		gr.	gr.	gr.	mg.	mg.	mg.	mg.	mg.		mg.	mg.	mg.
barley, pearled	1,583	37.2	4.5	357.4	73	857	9.1	14	726	(0)	.55	.23	14.1
buckwheat flour, dark	1,510	53.1	11.3	326.6	150	1,574	12.7	0	0	(0)	2.61	.68	13.2
cornmeal, degermed	1,651	35.8	5.4	355.6	27	449	5.0		544	2,000	.64	.23	4.5
farina	1,642	51.7	4.1	349.3	113	485	6.8	9	376	0	.27	.45	3.2
millet	1,483	44.9	13.2	330.7	91	1,411	30.8	0	1,950	(0)	3.30	1.70	10.6
oatmeal	1,769	64.4	33.6	309.4	240	1,837	20.4	9	1,597	(0)	2.72	.64	4.5
pancake mix, wheat	1,615	39.0	8.2	343.4	2,041	2,676	6.4	6,500	735	0	.54	.36	5.0
pancake mix, buckwheat	1,488	47.6	8.6	318.9	2,114	3,747	14.1	6,051	2,159	trace	1.63	.54	10.0
brown rice, raw	1,633	34.0	8.6	351.1	145	1,002	7.3	41	971	(0)	1.52	.24	21.4
rye, whole grain	1,515	54.9	7.7	332.9	(172)	1,706	16.8	(5)	2,118	(0)	1.94	1.02	7.1
dark rye flour	1,483	73.9	11.8	308.9	245	(2,431)	20.4	5	3,901	(0)	2.76	.98	12.2
sesame seeds, whole	2,640	82.6	242.2	79.8	499	2,685	10.9	0	0	0	.80	.59	24.5
soy beans, dry & raw	1,828	154.7	80.3	152.0	1,025	2,513	38.1	23	7,607	360	4.99	1.43	10.1
soy bean flour	1,910	166.5	92.1	137.9	903	2,531	38.1	5	7,530	500	3.85	1.41	9.6
sunflower seeds, hulled	2,540	108.9	214.6	90.3	544	3,797	32.2	136	4,173	230	8.90	1.05	24.7

	food energy calories	protein	fat	carbohydrates	calcium	phosphorus	iron	sodium	potassium	vitamin A units	thiamine	riboflavin	niacin
		gr.	gr.	gr.	mg.	mg.	mg.	mg.	mg.		mg.	mg.	mg.
hard spring wheat	1,495	63.5	10.0	313.4	163	1,737	14.1	(14)	1,678	(0)	2.59	.54	19.5
all-purpose wheat flour*	1,651	47.6	4.5	345.2	73	395	13.0	9	431	(0)	2.0	1.20	16.0
pastry flour	1,651	34.0	3.6	360.2	77	331	2.3	9	431	(0)	.14	.14	3.0
gluten flour	1,715	187.8	8.6	214.1	181	635	0	9	272	(0)	0	0	0
wheat bran	900	72.8	20.9	280.8	540	5,788	67.6	41	5,085	(0)	3.25	1.59	95.3
wheat germ	1,647	120.7	49.4	211.8	327	5,071	42.6	14	3,751	(0)	9.10	3.09	19.2
whole wheat flour	1,510	60.3	9.1	322.1	186	1,687	15.0	14	1,678	(0)	2.49	.54	19.7
wheat flakes	1,542	44.9	9.1	345.6	163	1,551	14.5	9	1,724	(0)	1.65	.55	18.6
whole wheat farina	1,533	61.2	9.1	328.0	204	1,805	16.8	9	1,678	(0)	2.30	.61	21.2

*enriched to maximum standards as required by law, 1970

source: *Composition of Foods*, Consumer and Food Economic Research Division, United States Department of Agriculture. Washington, D.C.

USEFUL MEASUREMENTS

food	quantity	yield
apples	1 medium	1 cup sliced
barley, pearl	1 cup uncooked	4 cups cooked
bread crumbs	3 to 4 slices	1 cup dry crumbs
brown sugar	1 pound	2¼ cups firmly packed
cabbage	1 pound	4 cups shredded
cheese	¼ pound	1 cup shredded
conectioners sugar	1 pound	3½ cups sifted
cornmeal	1 cup uncooked	4 cups cooked
crackers, soda	16	1 cup coarse crumbs
flour, all-purpose	1 pound	4 cups sifted
millet	1 cup uncooked	3¾ cups cooked
onion	1 medium	½ cup chopped
rice, brown	1 cup uncooked	3½ cups cooked
shortening	1 pound	2 cups
soy beans	1 cup uncooked	2¼ cups cooked
sugar, granulated	1 pound	2¼ cups
Stone-Buhr cereals	refer to Cereal Cooking chart on pages 17 and 18	

INDICES

These indices have been designed so that you can easily find what you are looking for.

The *Allergy Index* lists recipes that can be used in wheat, egg or milk free diets. Recipes that traditionally use milk, egg or wheat but have been modified to now exclude these ingredients are classified under the allergy index. There are many other recipes in this book that persons on restricted diets can use . . . they are not listed in the allergy section because they rarely contain wheat, milk or eggs. For more information, see the Allergy Recipe Information on page 16.

The *General Index* lists the recipes according to categories that fit into a meal such as breads or vegetables. The main dishes are classified according to the major ingredient, such as fish, poultry or ground meat. The desserts are divided and listed under the kind of dessert the recipe is for. For example, some of the headings under which you can find desserts are pies, cakes, cobblers and cookies.

The *Product Index* lists each grain product and the recipes that contain that product. This is so that when you purchase a grain product you can easily find many ways to use it. In addition to the recipes listed, be sure to see the chart, Varying the Grains You Use on page 82. This chart will tell you suggested ways to substitute many grain products in the recipes in this book. Have fun discovering the variety of ways that grains can add interest to your meals!

ALLERGY

GENERAL

PRODUCT

Barley Flakes 16,

162

please send me_____ copies of
cooking with GOURMET GRAINS
at $2.95 each washington state residents add sales tax
enclose your check, money order or
charge card number (on reverse)
postage prepaid by the Stone-Buhr
Milling Co.

name

street

city   state   zip

please send me_____ copies of
cooking with GOURMET GRAINS
at $2.95 each washington state residents add sales tax
enclose your check, money order or
charge card number (on reverse)
postage prepaid by the Stone-Buhr
Milling Co.

name

street

city   state   zip

please send me_____ copies of
cooking with GOURMET GRAINS
at $2.95 each washington state residents add sales tax
enclose your check, money order or
charge card number (on reverse)
postage prepaid by the Stone-Buhr
Milling Co.

name

street

city   state   zip

please send me_____ copies of
cooking with GOURMET GRAINS
at $2.95 each washington state residents add sales tax
enclose your check, money order or
charge card number (on reverse)
postage prepaid by the Stone-Buhr
Milling Co.

name

street

city   state   zip

master charge

card number

authorized signature   expiration date

bankamericard

card number

authorized signature   expiration date

mail to   Stone-Buhr Milling Co.
4052 28th Ave. S.W.
Seattle, Wash. 98126

---

master charge

card number

authorized signature   expiration date

bankamericard

card number

authorized signature   expiration date

mail to   Stone-Buhr Milling Co.
4052 28th Ave. S.W.
Seattle, Wash. 98126

---

master charge

card number

authorized signature   expiration date

bankamericard

card number

authorized signature   expiration date

mail to   Stone-Buhr Milling Co.
4052 28th Ave. S.W.
Seattle, Wash. 98126

---

master charge

card number

authorized signature   expiration date

bankamericard

card number

authorized signature   expiration date

mail to   Stone-Buhr Milling Co.
4052 28th Ave. S.W.
Seattle, Wash. 98126